DIXIE'S GREAT WAR

WAR, MEMORY, AND CULTURE

Series Editor
Steven Trout

Advisory Board
Joan Beaumont
Philip D. Beidler
John Bodnar
Patrick Hagopian
Mara Kozelsky
Edward T. Linenthal
Kendall R. Phillips
Kirk Savage
Jay Winter

Series published in cooperation with

THE CENTER FOR THE STUDY OF
WAR & MEMORY
at the UNIVERSITY OF SOUTH ALABAMA

www.southalabama.edu/departments/research/warandmemory
Susan McCready, Content Editor

DIXIE'S GREAT WAR

Edited by John M. Giggie and Andrew J. Huebner

Afterword by Jay Winter

The University of Alabama Press   Tuscaloosa

The University of Alabama Press
Tuscaloosa, Alabama 35487–0380
uapress.ua.edu

Inquiries about reproducing material from this work should
be addressed to the University of Alabama Press.

Typeface: Adobe Caslon Pro

Cover image: *Colored Man Is No Slacker*, WWI poster by
E. G. Renesch (1918)
Cover design: David Nees

Publication made possible in part through the generous
support of The Summersell Center for the Study of the
South at The University of Alabama.

Cataloging-in-Publication data is available from the Library of Congress.
ISBN: 978–0-8173–2072–0
E-ISBN: 978–0-8173–9327–4

Contents

Note on Audience Participation

In the interest of clarity and efficiency, we intervened lightly in editing questions and comments from audience members, filtering out repetition, conversational asides, and inaudible dialogue. We also preserved the anonymity of those participants. We did not, however, feel comfortable mediating or censoring the *content* of audience contributions, even when questioners used outdated or offensive language. Our goal was not to endorse such views, of course, but to provide an honest account of the opinions aired at the symposium. Finally, audience members occasionally made factual statements or used statistics that we could not verify but that we left in place, likewise to remain faithful to the day's proceedings.

Acknowledgments

The authors would like to thank the wonderful scholars who came to Tuscaloosa in October 2017 and then worked hard to refine their comments and move this volume to completion. But the symposium from which it sprung would not have been possible without the help of many other people: Sea Talantis, Lauren Lewis, Morta Riggs, Ellen Pledger, and Christina Kircharr. We would also like to recognize the financial support of institutional partners from the University of Alabama, including the Department of History, the Bankhead Fund, Dr. Lesley Gordon (Summersell Chair of Southern History), the Summersell Center for the Study of the South, the Graduate School, the Department of American Studies, the Department of English, the Office for Research and Economic Development, and Dean Robert Olin of the College of Arts and Sciences. Finally, we are grateful for the steady guidance of our editors at the University of Alabama Press: Claire Lewis Evans, senior acquisitions editor, and Dan Waterman, editor-in-chief.

DIXIE'S GREAT WAR

Introduction

JOHN M. GIGGIE AND ANDREW J. HUEBNER

On Friday, October 6, 2017, twelve scholars of the American experience in the First World War joined us in Tuscaloosa, Alabama, for a one-day symposium called Dixie's Great War. The workshop, open to the public as well as faculty, staff, and students at the University of Alabama, had two primary purposes, one commemorative and one interpretive. First, like organizers of other similar events around the country, we intended to draw attention to and remember the Great War during the centennial of American intervention. Second, we meant to explore iterations of the Great War experience in the American South and among southerners.

A few months ahead of the conference, we posed questions to our panelists for their consideration that would guide their opening remarks: How did the First World War affect the South and southerners in your particular area of expertise? How did the South or southern values and culture impact the wider war effort? Did southern soldiers experience the war, either in stateside camps or in Europe, in a particular way? We hoped all of these questions would drive the central one—was there a distinctive southern experience during the Great War?

The resulting conversations generated no singular historical argument or historiographical intervention but instead a dialogue—something rather in the spirit of the 2009 publication, *The Legacy of the Great War: Ninety Years On*, edited by Jay Winter, which itself grew out of a series of public scholars' forums. "We offer here a glimpse of how historians operate," Winter wrote in the preface to that collection, and we share that ambition in *Dixie's Great War*.[1] Our panelists prepared initial remarks but spent much of each session asking or reacting to questions and extrapolating on earlier points. Indeed, this volume seeks to capture the process of historians at work with the public, pushing and probing general understandings of the past. As both producers and readers of Great War scholarship, of course, their interchanges engaged with the broader literature on the American experience in the conflict.

While the panelists offered no unanimous conclusions to our prompts, their replies did circle around a particular concept: southern exceptionalism or the prospect that the South and its residents experienced and participated in American history in fundamentally unique ways. The term *southern exceptionalism* has a long and complicated history. For many white historians writing before the civil rights movement, the term signaled the honorable character of white southerners and their institutions. It too often included a portrayal of slavery as a positive good, the Civil War as the product of northern aggression, and segregation as a necessary restoration of political and social order. Long after such assumptions were debunked and discarded, southern exceptionalism persisted in a different form to influence the popular telling of America's history in the twentieth century and, more particularly, the story of modern struggles for racial justice. Southern exceptionalists of this stripe assumed that the nation's crisis over civil rights was centered in Dixie to the near exclusion of activities in the North or Midwest. Similarly, they located the development of the conservative counterrevolution of the 1970s in southern and suburban disaffection with political liberalism.[2]

In contrast to these historical conceptions of southern exceptionalism, scholars of the current generation generally view the story of the South as deeply integrated into the broader unfolding of national tensions and crises. While the region certainly features distinctions of, say, economy and demography, those distinctions hardly qualify as exceptional. Put more bluntly, they tend to argue for, in the titles of two fairly recent publications, *The End of Southern Exceptionalism* and *The Myth of Southern Exceptionalism*.[3]

Yet the question of whether and to what degree the South understood and experienced the Great War in particular ways remains an open one. For at the outbreak of hostilities, the South, when compared to other regions of the nation, was indeed more rural, its economy more agricultural, its people poorer and less ethnically diverse, and its systems of public health, transportation, and education less developed. Most of the country's lynchings had occurred, and would continue to occur, in the region. How did these characteristics affect the wartime lives of southerners? The answers offered by the scholars in this volume do not collectively reassert the detachment of the South from American life but instead argue for a relationship of reciprocal influence between region and nation.

We organized the twelve participants into four panels. Jennifer D. Keene, Ross A. Kennedy, and Michael S. Neiberg started the symposium with a session called "Mobilizing for the Great War." Then came "Fighting the Great War Over Here," featuring Jessica L. Adler, Nancy K. Bristow, and Martin "Marty" T. Olliff. Next was a panel with Ruth Smith Truss, Kara Dixon Vuic, and Chad L. Williams on "Fighting the Great War Over There." Finally, the last session was "Finding Meaning in the Great War" with Jonathan H. Ebel, Derryn Moten, and Steven Trout. We asked our guests to keep their remarks brief and to leave ample time for audience questions. Although we gave these scholars an opportunity to lightly edit their remarks after the conference, our intention was to preserve an interactive and conversational tone. We hope, then, that this collection offers a faithful representation of that day's dynamic effort by twelve academics and an audience to discuss, debate, and characterize the experience of the South and southerners during the Great War era.

When reviewing the thoughts of our panelists and audience members after the fact, it became evident that the South evoked during the conference was not comprehensive. It included former Confederate states Alabama, Arkansas, Georgia, Mississippi, Tennessee, North and South Carolina, and Virginia—but not Texas, Florida, and Louisiana. Our discussion also tended to concentrate on certain types of southerners: black and white, rich and poor, male and female. Generally absent were Mexican Americans, Native Americans, and Asian Americans. These exceptions to what constituted the South and southerners clearly limit the representative nature of the conclusions we reach in this volume, though our ambition was never to make definitive judgments about the South as a whole and its relationship to the Great War. Instead, we strove to look at critical cross sections of the South and its populations and raise new queries about connections between region and nation during the years of conflict.

To that point, none of our invited panelists argued for an absolutely unique southern experience. Rather, they shared three general and overlapping approaches to the question of wartime exceptionalism. First, several speakers cautiously advanced the idea that southerners felt the war differently from others. Some pointed out that antimilitarism was especially rampant in the South (and among prominent southern politicians), with a regional suspicion both of the central government and of northern industrialists who stood to gain by the war in a way southern agriculture did not. Everyone granted, however, that the Midwest and Plains states saw similar resistance. The same could be said of the way southerners experienced America's first major national conscription and the influenza pandemic. Isolated, rural, or poor men might run afoul of the draft boards or have their draft calls manipulated by landowners, and such men were high in number in the South. Most African American men lived in the South, so their experience of being drafted disproportionately might be thought of as peculiarly southern in a way. But white supremacy was hardly confined to the former Confederate states and influenced national policy as well as the contours of black life during the war. Southerners likewise suffered terribly from the flu, and black southerners faced a segregated and substandard medical care system. But perhaps these southern trials owed less to regional idiosyncrasies and more to rural isolation, underdeveloped health care, and poverty.

Second, many speakers argued that one of the First World War's signature effects was to flatten regional differences in favor of a national experience, pointing especially to the widening reach of the federal government and the development of a national war effort. The war provoked the growth of a federally controlled veterans' medical system that nationalized care from New York City to the Deep South and beyond. Southern states lobbied to bring federal training camps and their concomitant economic advantages to Dixie. Once drafted, selectmen served alongside men of their own regions for a time, but many encountered soldiers from all over the country once the divisions got organized and then shuffled and reshuffled in training and in France. Combat meant shared hardships for soldiers regardless of regional origins. And black southern soldiers met black northerners as well as Africans in France, broadening their sense of racial consciousness and building a common experience of freedoms greater and more varied than those found at home.

Third, many panelists suggested that rather than simply differing from or resembling the national experience—both of which imply a sort of separation between Dixie and the rest of the country—the South and southerners *shaped* that broader story of America's Great War, not least because Woodrow Wilson and others from the region occupied positions of national authority on a scale not seen in several generations. Participants noted that the war accelerated, though did not create, an impulse to generate national unity by celebrating Confederate military heritage. A big part of the national draft registration days, as well as the broader ethos of the war in the South, was to summon, urge, or reignite southern martial virtue. Lost Cause sentimentalism was everywhere in southern wartime culture. Federal authorities named training camps after Nathan Bedford Forrest and other Confederate luminaries. Related to that pattern, the most dramatic southern wartime influence came in race relations. Southerners had no monopoly on white supremacy, but our speakers argued that southerners' passionate fears about black men in uniform and their supposed sexual degradation, along with white southern commitment to racial segregation and injustice, shaped national policy stateside and in France. White southerners had a friend in Wilson and other powerful figures in the federal government, who aggressively blocked black leaders and sympathetic white commanders who demanded black combat soldiers, integrated units, and a proportional black officer corps. Secretary of War Newton Baker, a progressive northerner, buckled to pressure from Dixie to keep the army segregated and black troops in service roles, despite the creation of two all-black combat divisions that in turn attracted unfounded criticism from Sen. James Vardaman of Mississippi and other prominent white supremacists. Black soldiers in France mingled somewhat freely with French women until white southerners and other military officials stopped it. Authorities exported Jim Crow "justice" when they hanged a disproportionate number of black soldiers accused of committing rape. Then southern segregationists successfully applied racial apartheid to the veterans' health care system and postwar veterans' advocacy organizations.

These arguments and points of emphasis, in turn, join a larger conversation about the South during the First World War. Produced during the greater centennial moment, that scholarship collectively reveals the same range of particular and universal experiences that our panelists charted and the same symbiotic relationship between southern values and the national war story. Some works go further in tracing how the war, in turn, transformed the South, just as much of the broader Americanist literature on the Great War has tracked the durable impact of that conflict on the twentieth- and twenty-first century United States.[4]

The overlapping matters of particular and universal experience, of reciprocal influence between the national war effort and the South, and of the war's long and underappreciated shadow—all weave through a collection called *The American South and the Great War, 1914–1924*, edited by Matthew Downs and M. Ryan Floyd. Essays in that volume show North Carolinians setting aside sectionalism in favor of national obligation, federal trade policies with Britain affected by the politics of cotton cultivation in Alabama, attempts to rally support in South Carolina running up against persistent opposition to the intervention, southerners' efforts to convert the national emergency into regional industrial development, and the Food Administration's regulatory marginalization of southern farmers. These writers and many others operate in territory charted earlier by scholars including David Kennedy, Joseph Fry, Christopher Capozzola, Jeannette Keith, Gerald Shenk, and Jennifer Keene, who have scrutinized the ways southerners and other Americans either resisted, acquiesced to, or capitalized upon the rising power and reach of the federal state.[5] Those poles of support and dissent are also the subject, respectively, of two recent works on the national (including southern) scene: Michael S. Neiberg's *The Path to War* and Michael Kazin's *War against War*. Other contributors in the Downs and Floyd volume follow the ways new demands for national wartime service alternately facilitated or undermined southern movements for gender and racial equality. Like many historians and some of our panelists, these authors argue that the Great War environment brought no immediate sea change to gender and race relations—and in fact, as noted above, featured an ascendant white supremacy—but rather generated an emboldened activism that would intensify later.[6]

Other works have dug more deeply into subjects that emerged during our symposium (and many others that did not) across the various states of the American South. In the aggregate, these books aim to commemorate the service of citizens in the various states, put their experiences into the context of the national story, and demonstrate the war's tremendous impact on the South. Our participant Martin Olliff edited a collection called *The Great War in the Heart of Dixie: Alabama during World War I*. Olliff's authors directed their attention to many of the topics that drove the later Downs and Floyd volume and some additional ones. These include the impact of the national mobilization on southern communities where training cantonments were located, as well as the wartime infrastructural improvements that fueled a temporary economic boom in Mobile. Authors also addressed support for the war, both among white women in Montgomery and, for very different reasons, among African American church leaders as a (for now, unrealized) path to civil rights. Contributors looked at white resentment of the war-driven northward black migration, as well as the drafting and arming of black men, the draft's exposure of public health problems in Alabama, and that state's subsequent role in addressing them. Also discussed were patriotic efforts by local organizations and later attempts to memorialize Alabama's wartime sacrifices. (*Dixie's Great War* participant Steven Trout focused sustained attention on commemoration, including in the South and among southern writers, in *On the Battlefield of Memory: The First World War and American Remembrance, 1919–1941*.) Another essay in the Olliff volume, by our panelist Ruth Truss, explored the training and combat experiences of the state's four infantry regiments, similar to Nimrod Frazer's project *Send the Alabamians: World War I Fighters in the Rainbow Division*. Soldiers from other states have had their stories told in Gregory Bell's *They Called Them Soldier Boys: A Texas Infantry Regiment in World War I*; by Edward A. Gutiérrez in *Doughboys on the Great War: How American Soldiers Viewed Their Military Experience*, which features Virginia soldiers among those of three other states; and in Anne L. Webster's *Mississippians in the Great War: Selected Letters*, a collection of correspondence from soldiers, nurses, and YMCA workers.

Across these subjects of home front mobilization, soldier deployment, and postwar memorialization and change, several other works on southern states have added cumulative strength to the broader narrative of the region: a place whose institutions and connection to the federal state were transformed by the war, a place where women and people of color keyed wartime service to citizenship claims despite the grip of bigotry and tradition, a place where conscription revealed the tension between martial honor and duty on one hand and antistatist dissent and lingering Lost Cause resentments on the other. These works—which include Lynn Rainville's *Virginia and the Great War*, Shepherd W. McKinley and Steven Sabol's *North Carolina's Experience during the First World War*, Michael D. Polston and Guy Lancaster's *To Can the Kaiser: Arkansas and the Great War*, and David J. Bettez's *Kentucky and the Great War: World War I on the Home Front*—largely follow the model of the earlier Olliff volume, charting local religious responses to the war, local handling of the influenza epidemic, local people's experiences at the front and at home, and local reverberations of wartime mobilization. All these volumes also track local expressions of patriotism, dissent, and anti-German hysteria, which Christopher C. Gibbs explored in a border state in *The Great Silent Majority: Missouri's Resistance to World War I*, and which Matthew D. Tippens examined more recently in *Turning Germans into Texans*.

Following in the footsteps of many of these books, our volume attempts to evoke the particular and national dimensions to the question of how the South and southerners participated in the war. It joins as well a broad public interest in remembering the Great War during its centennial period. This culture of commemoration, however, has been episodic and geographically varied. At the international level, countries including Great Britain, France, and Germany developed national programming that gripped citizens across Europe. British artist Rob Heard unveiled his massive public art project, *Shrouds of the Somme*, at Queen Elizabeth Olympic Park in London on November 7, 2018. Heard crafted 72,396 statues, each a twelve-inch human figure painted white and tightly shrouded in a burial cloth of sorts. The number of statues matches the total number of British and Commonwealth soldiers with no known grave killed in action during the Battle of the Somme in 1916. Over a million soldiers died or were wounded during this four-month clash waged by the British and French against the Germans. Heard and members of the Royal Anglian Regiment lay out the statues in a tight grid that covered 43,000 square feet. Tens of thousands lined up to see the exhibit.[7] To mark the formal signing of the November 1918 armistice between the Allies and Germany in Compiègne, French president Emmanuel Macron met German chancellor Angela Merkel in this small town exactly one hundred years later. They held hands to symbolize their mutual commitment to peace. The next day Macron hosted over seventy world leaders in a ceremony at the Arc de Triomphe, recalling the lives of the ten million who died during the conflict. He took the opportunity to remind his audience that the lasting meaning of war must be an unwavering commitment to peace. "History sometimes threatens to repeat its tragic patterns," Macron said, "and undermine the legacy of peace we thought we had sealed with the blood of our ancestors."[8]

By contrast, large-scale American efforts of the type that took place in Europe sometimes struggled to take shape. In 2012, Pres. Barack Obama signed into law a bill creating the World War One Centennial Commission, whose principle objective was to open a memorial in time for the war's centennial, but fundraising problems and political infighting over the design have delayed completion until at least 2021.[9] The main national site of remembrance remains the National World War I Museum and Memorial in Kansas City, Missouri, dedicated in 1926 but only designated by Congress as the national memorial in the twenty-first century. It ran a series of popular exhibits in 2018 and 2019, including *Images of the Great War: America Crosses the Atlantic*.[10] The Smithsonian's National Museum of Natural History marked the anniversary with a new exhibition, *Outbreak: Epidemics in a Connected World*. It considered how the influenza pandemic affected America and the world during the war and beyond.[11]

But for most Americans, the First World War has proven resistant to the sort of dramatic popular narratives that have driven commemoration of other wars. World War II continues to serve as a beacon of purpose and resolve in American culture, its vast scope and tangled origins usually boiled down to triumphant stories of good over evil, democracy over fascism, freedom over slavery. Although the Korean War remains quiet in the country's historical memory, the larger Cold War of which it was a part still bears some of the moral certainty of the Second World War, just as charges of socialism remain potent in the American political arena. The Civil War endures in the collective imagination not only as a drama of sectional, even familial, conflict but also because its contested meanings continue to carry water for present-day causes and antipathies—sometimes with deadly results as in Charleston in 2015 and Charlottesville two years later. The Vietnam War cast a long shadow on American culture, politics, and foreign policy in the decades after the fall of Saigon, not for any summoning of unity like in World War II but for its exposure of deep rifts over the role of the United States in the world and the conduct of the American military. Vietnam brought a "reckoning," as one popular history recently put it, with cynicism and doubt and tragedy driving national storytelling just as their opposites drive storytelling about the Second World War.[12] The Great War offers most Americans no such simple, digestible interpretive clarity, whether uplifting or demoralizing. Around the world the First World War ended empires and redrew maps, and at home, it accelerated or provoked or impeded changes in racial and gender relations, understandings of citizenship, and the role of the federal state. But those transformations have failed to generate the same cinematic or commemorative possibilities of America's other great wars.

Whatever the war's shortage of galvanizing meaning, however, it demanded sacrifices of people across the country (even if those sacrifices paled next to those asked of other national populations), and thus state-based initiatives have enjoyed comparatively greater success than countrywide ones. Historical societies, universities, libraries, state commemoration commissions, and other local entities have drawn attention to the contributions of local citizens and the enduring impact of the war on communities. Also important to this commemorative energy has been the surge of interest in genealogy, made possible in large part by the digitization of census as well as military and demographic records, ever expanding public access to the Internet, and the emergence of websites like Ancestry.com, FindMyPast.com, Fold3.com, and FamilyHistorySearch.com. It is easier than ever to track the lives of ancestors during wartime.

Alabama offers a good example of local commemorative efforts. The state formed a fifty-three-member World War I Centennial Commission composed of educators, historians, archivists, librarians, politicians, business leaders, and private citizens. Helming the group were two state leaders: Steve Murray, director of the Alabama Department of Archives and History, and Maj. Gen. Sheryl E. Gordon, adjutant general of the Alabama National Guard. The commission supported conferences and museum exhibits and, on its website, catalogued Great War monuments, memorials, and historic sites erected across the state, offered a bibliography and lesson plans about how to teach the war to school children, and publicized community events. Among its most important functions was to organize a public blog cataloging the lives of forgotten men and women in the war like Priv. Owen Fowler, the son of a former slave who served in the segregated Ninety-Second Division and was mortally wounded in France only hours before the armistice. He was one of the final casualties among the nearly 2,500 Alabamians killed in the war.[13]

Operating in similar function and leading their own states' commemorative activities were the Tennessee Great War Commission, the North Carolina Museum of History, the Georgia World War I Centennial Commission, the Florida World War I Centennial Commission, the Virginia World War I Commemoration Commission, and comparable bodies in nonsouthern states.[14] Texas was exemplary: its centennial commission created TexasTimeTravel.com, a virtual tour of Great War historical sites in Texas, and *Texas and the Great War Travel Guide*, a short history of the role of the state's towns and cities in the war effort.[15] In Louisiana, the Historical New Orleans Collection and Southeastern Louisiana University hosted exhibits and speakers.[16]

Our volume shares the twin purpose of these efforts—to study and to commemorate. It engages without seeking to close the question of southern exceptionalism. In its conversational tone and mix of professional and public voices, it aspires as well to model a community conversation about the meaning of the war and encourages acts of civic engagement. Such acts could include recording family stories about the war, preserving community histories, and contributing to broader efforts to build archival collections so critical for future generations of historians. Another would be to simply locate local memorials—statues, historical markers, buildings—and try to understand why they were erected. The physical landscape of the campus at the University of Alabama, for example, was fundamentally transformed by commemorative efforts. Overall, 2,254 students and alumni of the university served in the war. Forty-five residents of Tuscaloosa County lost their lives. Several years after the armistice, university leaders memorialized the dead by planting forty-five oak trees along University Boulevard.[17] More recently, officials installed a small marker bearing each name near the Denny Chimes bell tower.

Today no student can walk across campus and not pass these trees, though we wonder if they fully grasp their significance. Learning about such acts of public remembrance, whether in Tuscaloosa or in thousands of other places across the country with similar tributes, prompts us to think about how the First World War revealed and provoked transformations in human experience that remain visible, if often unrecognized, to this day.

NOTES

1. Jay Winter, ed., *The Legacy of the Great War: Ninety Years On* (Columbia: University of Missouri Press, 2009), xi.

2. For a summary of the literature on southern exceptionalism, see Matthew Lassiter and Joseph Crespino, eds., *The Myth of Southern Exceptionalism* (New York: Oxford University Press, 2010); and Dan Carter, "Is There a South and Does It Still Matter," *Dissent* 54, no. 3 (Summer 2007): 92–96. W. E. B. Du Bois attacked the popular fantasy of southern exceptionalism in *Black Reconstruction in America: A History of the Part Which Black Folks Played in the Attempt to Reconstruct Democracy in America, 1860–1880* (New York: Harcourt, Brace, 1935). See also John Hope Franklin, *From Slavery to Freedom: A History of the American Negro* (New York: Alfred A. Knopf, 1947); and C. Vann Woodward, *Origins of the New South* (Baton Rouge: Louisiana State University Press, 1981).

3. Lassiter and Crespino, *Myth of Southern Exceptionalism*; and Byron E. Schafer and Richard Johnson, eds., *The End of Southern Exceptionalism: Class, Race, and Partisan Change in the Postwar South* (Cambridge, MA: Harvard University Press, 2006).

4. For works by *Dixie's Great War* participants who share this ambition to elevate the war in American history, see Nancy K. Bristow, *Making Men Moral: Social Engineering during the*

Great War (New York: New York University Press, 1996); Jennifer D. Keene, *Doughboys, The Great War, and the Remaking of America* (Baltimore: Johns Hopkins University Press, 2001); Martin T. Olliff, ed., *The Great War in the Heart of Dixie: Alabama during World War I* (Tuscaloosa: University of Alabama Press, 2008); Ross A. Kennedy, *The Will to Believe: Woodrow Wilson, World War I, and America's Strategy for Peace and Security* (Kent, OH: Kent State University Press, 2009); Jonathan H. Ebel, *Faith in the Fight: Religion and the American Soldier in the Great War* (Princeton, NJ: Princeton University Press, 2010); Steven Trout, *On the Battlefield of Memory: The First World War and American Remembrance, 1919–1941* (Tuscaloosa: University of Alabama Press, 2010); Chad L. Williams, *Torchbearers of Democracy: African American Soldiers in the World War I Era* (Chapel Hill: University of North Carolina Press, 2010); Michael S. Neiberg, *The Path to War: How the First World War Created Modern America* (New York: Oxford University Press, 2016); Jessica L. Adler, *Burdens of War: Creating the United States Veterans Health System* (Baltimore: Johns Hopkins University Press, 2017); Andrew J. Huebner, *Love and Death in the Great War* (New York: Oxford University Press, 2018); Kara Dixon Vuic, *The Girls Next Door: Bringing the Home Front to the Front Lines* (Cambridge, MA: Harvard University Press, 2019).

5. See David M. Kennedy, *Over Here: The First World War and American Society* (New York: Oxford University Press, 2004 ed.); Joseph A. Fry, *Dixie Looks Abroad: The South and U.S. Foreign Relations, 1789–1973* (Baton Rouge: Louisiana State University Press, 2002); Christopher Capozzola, *Uncle Sam Wants You: World War I and the Making of the Modern American Citizen* (New York: Oxford University Press, 2008); Jeanette Keith, *Rich Man's War, Poor Man's Fight: Race, Class, and Power in the Rural South during the First World War* (Chapel Hill: University of North Carolina Press, 2004); Gerald E. Shenk, *"Work or Fight!": Race, Gender, and the Draft in World War One* (New York: Palgrave Macmillan, 2005); Keene, *Doughboys*.

6. See, for example, Williams, *Torchbearers of Democracy*; Vuic, *Girls Next Door*; Lettie Gavin, *American Women in World War I: They Also Served* (Boulder: University Press of Colorado, 1997); Kimberly Jensen, *Mobilizing Minerva: American Women in the First World War* (Urbana: University of Illinois Press, 2008); Susan Zeiger, *In Uncle Sam's Service: Women Workers with the American Expeditionary Force, 1917–1919* (Ithaca, NY: Cornell University Press, 1999).

7. *Shrouds of the Somme*, www.shroudsofthesomme.com; Alan Taylor, "Preparing for the Centenary of the End of World War I," *Atlantic*, November 7, 2018, www.theatlantic.com; "Shrouds of the Somme Exhibit Comes to Olympic Park," British Broadcasting News, November 7, 2018, www.bbc.com; "'Saluting, Crying, Praying'—Emotional Response to Somme Art," British Broadcasting News, August 23, 2018, www.bbc.com; Steve Wright, "Bristol Cathedral Hosts Shrouds of the Somme," B24/7, October 1, 2016, www.bristol247.com.

8. "In Solemn Paris Ceremony, Macron Leads Global WWI Armistice Commemorations," *Reuters World News*, November 10, 2018, www.reuters.com.

9. On the national war memorial, see United States World War One Centennial Commission, www.worldwar1centennial.org. For controversies surrounding it, see Philip Kennicott, "America Is Chock-Full of World War I Memorials, So Why Build Another?"

Washington Post, January 23, 2016, www.washingtonpost.com; Michele Lefrak, "Why a National World War I Memorial Still Doesn't Exist in Washington," WAMU American University Radio, November 12, 2018, wamu.org; and Blake Paterson, "Washington's Battle for a World War I Memorial, *Politico*, May 28, 2018, www.politico.com.

10. National WWI Museum and Memorial, *Images of the Great War*, www.theworldwar.org.

11. Smithsonian Institution, *Outbreak: Epidemics in a Connected World*, www.si.edu.

12. See Christian G. Appy, *American Reckoning: The Vietnam War and Our National Identity* (New York: Viking, 2015).

13. Interview with Steve Murray, June 25, 2018. United States World War One Centennial Commission, "Alabama in World War I," www.worldwar1centennial.org/index.php/alabama-in-wwi-home.html.

14. On Tennessee, see Tennessee Great War Commission, tnsos.net/TSLA/GWC; on North Carolina, see North Carolina Museum of History, "World War I Centennial Commemoration," www.ncmuseumofhistory.org; on Georgia, see United States World War One Centennial Commission, "Georgia World War I Centennial Commission," www.worldwar1centennial.org; on Florida, see United States World War One Centennial Commission, "Floridians Who Served over There," www.worldwar1centennial.org; on Virginia, see Virginia WWI and WWII Commission, www.virginiawwiandwwii.org. See also United States World War One Centennial Commission, "California in World War I," www.worldwar1centennial.org, and Over There: Missouri and the Great War, missourioverthere.org.

15. See the Texas Historical Commission, "World War I Centennial," and "Texas and the Great War," www.thc.texas.gov.

16. For the Historical New Orleans Collection, see www.hnoc.org. For Southeastern Louisiana University, see "The Center for Southeast Louisiana Studies at Southeastern to Host Exhibit Commemorating World War I Centennial," www.southeastern.edu.

17. Matthew Culver, "The University of Alabama in World War I," Summersell Center for the Study of the South, summersell.ua.edu.

I

Mobilizing for the Great War

Jennifer D. Keene, Ross A. Kennedy, and Michael S. Neiberg

The First World War required an unprecedented mobilization of resources, opinion, and people in 1917 and 1918. Across remarks on the debates over conscription, the shaping of policy, trade with Europe, race and ethnicity, regional antimilitarism, and life in the training camps, Jennifer Keene, Ross Kennedy, and Michael Neiberg collectively posited a modestly distinctive southern experience but with important qualifications and limits. Audience members asked the panelists for further discussion of definitions—of "the South" and "the Great War"—and for their thoughts on regional animosities, sectional reconciliation, the preparedness debate, and the role of southern churches in the war mobilization.

MICHAEL NEIBERG: I'm going to discuss the question of a distinctive southern response to the war in Europe from 1914 to 1917. Thinking about this took me back to the five years that I taught at the University of Southern Mississippi. When we were building our own center for the study of war and society, this was a question we kept coming back to. Is there a distinctive southern relationship to war and to the military? If there is, when did it start, and if it exists, what are its distinctive characteristics? And is there a link to the First World War, or is the distinctive link between the South and the military (if it exists at all) a product of a later era?

One caveat before I get started: I am not a historian of the American South, so take whatever I'm about to say here with a grain of salt. Still, I think we can toss out two arguments at least that seem to be sort of out in the conventional wisdom.

First, when looking at newspaper responses, when looking at the responses of community leaders, letters, memoirs, diaries, there doesn't seem to me to be any significant qualitative difference between the response of southerners and the response of northerners to events like the outbreak of the war, the sinking of the *Lusitania*, the torpedoing of the *Sussex*, the Zimmermann Telegram, or any other major events. Southern reactions and northern reactions are more or less the same.

Second, it is hard to argue that this was a regional government—that is, a northern government—setting policy. The Wilson cabinet was disproportionally southern. Wilson himself of course was a southerner and proud of it, even if he ran for president from New Jersey. His close adviser Edward House was a Texan. Walter Hines Page, his ambassador to Great Britain and an extremely influential person, was from Pinehurst, North Carolina. Josephus Daniels was also from North Carolina. I could go on and on and on. From a very brief glance at any rate, many of the early American volunteers who went to Europe to fight for either the British or the French or those who volunteered to go as nurses were also largely southern. And some of the most famous in their day included people like James McConnell and Kiffin Rockwell, both from Tennessee, who volunteered to fly in the Lafayette Escadrille, the pilots who flew for France. And in a little town called Carthage, North Carolina, there is a monument to McConnell, who was killed fighting for France.

So why am I here if my beginning argument is that there may not be that much difference? I think there are three avenues we could fruitfully explore.

The first is the nature of the southern economy, which, although it was industrializing in the late nineteenth and early twentieth centuries, was still predominantly agricultural and was still disproportionately related to the cotton industry, which became really important at the outbreak of the First World War. The First World War destroyed the global cotton market. In October 1913, the US South exported 250,000 bales of cotton. In October 1914, the South only exported 21,000 bales of cotton. The price of cotton itself dropped by more than 50 percent. I think you could make a pretty good case that the South's cotton economy never did recover from the global economic shock of 1914. The important point is that cotton became an extremely controversial topic between the United States and Great Britain for a kind of strange reason. Cotton was used by armies to put in between layers of artillery shells when they packed and shipped them so that the shells didn't knock together and accidentally blow up. So, for that reason, the Royal Navy and the British army wanted the British government, the Board of Trade in Great Britain, to declare cotton a contraband, in other words, something that it could seize as a war good. That obviously put what Great Britain wanted to do in some conflict with what the United States—especially the US South—wanted to do. As a result, there were two ongoing debates. One was inside the British government where the army and navy said, "Look, we're going to seize all the cotton coming out of the United States, and we're going to declare it contraband, and any American company that participates in the sale of cotton overseas (to anybody but us, of course) we're going to blacklist and do no business with them." On the other hand, the British government and the British ambassador to the United States, a man by the name of Sir Cecil Spring Rice, said, "Look, it's not worth the fight with the Americans over cotton. Let the cotton go through in order to keep relations with the United States healthy." And that debate went on well into 1916 when the British finally made the decision to let the cotton go through and not declare it as contraband. What this means in the United States, however, is to the extent that there was anti-British sentiment in the United States, much of it was based in southern rural economies that depended on cotton. And Sen. Hoke Smith of Georgia was the guy who became the kind of point man for this, and Claude Kitchin, a senator from North Carolina, emerged as a critical ally to him. They argued that Great Britain was using the war to unduly punish the American South. I want to stress that being anti-British did not necessarily equate in 1914, '15, or '16 with being pro-German. What it meant was that these senators wanted to push the US government to lean on the British to get rid of that contraband policy.

So the South did experience, it seems to me, more extended periods of anti-British sentiment than you see in the Northeast. Smith and Kitchin also both opposed any version of preparedness for war in 1915 and 1916 that would disproportionately move money from the South to the North. That is, they saw government grants to northern industry as being a way to use the war as an excuse to increase the power of the northeastern elite. By late 1916, as I noted, Great Britain gave up this cotton contraband policy, opting instead to buy southern cotton whenever it could and also increasing the amount of southern tobacco that it purchased in order to try to smooth some ruffled feathers over this issue. And by late 1916, Smith and Kitchin had both become, I think, out of step with where most Americans and most southern Americans were moving by the end of 1916, early 1917.

The second factor that I want to raise here is the ethnic makeup of the South, which is of course different, and this is a complicated topic that I cover in my book *The Path to War*. I'm just going to cover it very briefly here. In the North, there are four groups of people I examine, among others: Jewish Americans, Italian Americans, Irish Americans, and German Americans—and yes, I know all of those groups exist in the South, but they exist in larger concentrations in the North. All four of those groups in 1914 had their own reasons inside their communities to be either pro-German or anti-British. For the Irish, anger over British refusal to implement Home Rule for Ireland led to an initial suspicion of British motives. For most American Jews, the initial support went to Germany because they saw the German army and Austro-Hungarian army as certainly better than the Russian army, which served the most anti-Semitic country in Europe, and even better in some cases than the French, who had just come through the Dreyfus Affair. For Italian Americans, the entry of Italy into the war coincided roughly with American anger over the sinking of the *Lusitania.* What I argue in my book is that between 1914 and late 1916, each of these ethnic groups moved from an anti-British or pro-German position to a pro-Ally position, each for reasons internal to themselves but consistent with the wider American pattern. For Jews, this involved the behavior of the German army as it moved east through Jewish communities in Poland. It involved things like the Balfour Declaration issued by the British government. For Italians, of course, it was because Italy declared war in May 1915. The Irish and Germans are really complicated cases, but German Americans were disproportionately non-Prussian and Catholic, so their argument eventually became by late 1916, early 1917, that if Wilson's war was to be the war that Wilson claimed it would be, a war for democracy even in places like Germany, then it was a war that they could fight. If it was a war to destroy Germany, they couldn't. My only point in bringing this up is that this was a shift that happened in the North that I'm not sure happened in the South quite to the same extent. There was a convergence, I argue in *Path to War*, as all of these groups shifted from opposition to Great Britain or even support for Germany and Austria-Hungary in 1914 to a generally pro-Allied position by the end of 1916 and early 1917. Driving the shifts were factors internal to each community more than pressure from Washington. And again, that's not universal but broadly true.

The third factor that I want to bring up is the Great Migration, and here I'm certainly not an expert and I want to thank Chad Williams for helping me think through this. The Great Migration of course impacted the North as it impacted the South, but it had a particular impact here in the American South. The events of 1914 and 1915 effectively ended the mass waves of immigration from Europe into the United States, which meant that two patterns were going on inside the American South and inside the American economy more generally. One, there was an increased demand for labor, and two, there was a reduction in the labor source coming from Europe. What that meant of course for African Americans was an opportunity to leave the agricultural South and move first to the urban South and then have an opportunity, if they wished, to go to the urban North, which had a dramatic impact on southern society. Norfolk, Virginia, is probably the most important example. Because of its harbor, its strategic location, it saw an unbelievable expansion. The African American population of Norfolk between 1910 and 1920 rose 73 percent. Birmingham, Alabama's went up by 34 percent, Houston by a similar number. So this is the first kind of process that was happening, and most of this, I think, was happening before the United States entered the war. That is, it was happening as the economy was expanding and labor was contracting. So just to give you an idea, the *Chicago Defender* wrote that this process would give African American workers access to jobs they should have had all along but were denied because of European immigration. So this was a movement happening inside the South that eventually impacted the North, but in this early phase, 1914 to '16 or '17, it was impacting the South much more I think than it was impacting the North.

To sum up, we do see some differences at the margin, but I'm not convinced after having worked on the book and having thought about this for a couple of years at Southern Miss that it was World War I that began to set the distinctive pattern of southern interaction with the military. My guess is, without having done a whole lot of research on this, that this was a product of the all-volunteer force of the post-1973 age when the draft was no longer functioning to bring people into the military more or less equitably from all corners of the United States. So after 1973, when the United States went to a volunteer system, the one we have now, it was operating on market principles, which meant that regions like the American South, which were economically less developed, were going to produce larger numbers of people to commit to the military. The army did studies on this in the early 1970s, and the marines did too, intentionally targeting areas where they expected to find economically disadvantaged people. This meant inner cities, it meant the American Southwest, and it certainly meant targeting the American Southeast. In the 1960s and 1970s, the army and the navy and the air force were intentionally coming down into the South, closing ROTC programs in the North and opening them at branch campuses in the American South for exactly this reason. In other words, if you want to think of it in pure market terms, they're going where the supply is. And that's a problem that's much more a post-1973 one than it is a World War I problem.

So for this period, I think if you were living in Niagara Falls, New York, you actually had more in common with Tuscaloosa, Alabama, than you did with Niagara Falls, Ontario, just across the river. The big difference is between the United States and Canada, which was then of course part of the British Empire, whose wartime dynamic was different from the US dynamic. The differences within the United States are there, but it seems to me they're marginal.

ROSS KENNEDY: My task here is to address this question: How did the South or southern values impact the wider war effort? What I want to talk about is one part of white southern political ideology and how it affected America's involvement in the war. And the part I want to focus on in that ideology is the suspicion of large-scale standing armies, a kind of antimilitarist outlook that existed quite widely in the United States, especially in the South, in 1914.[1] So I'll break down the components of this train of thought and then talk a little bit about how I think it affected America's involvement in the war.

Antimilitarism included the suspicion that big armies, large-scale standing armies, would just enrich munitions makers, enrich big corporations, enrich bankers, and empower military officers, all of whom were seen by progressives (particularly agrarian ones) as opposed to progressive reform. In this way of thinking, militarists would use war scares and agitations for large-scale defense budgets, what they called "preparedness," to divert money and attention away from reform efforts. Another component of this hostility to big armies is that Americans associated them with monarchies, with Europe, with executive tyranny, and with overseas, imperialistic adventures that benefited elites. A third component is that large-scale armies were associated with high taxes that diminished economic opportunity for farmers and workers. Finally, the last strand combined a belief that local militias were the best way to fight wars (because you fought with your neighbors) with a distrust of distant military forces and an unwillingness to join them to defend your community.

As I mentioned, antimilitarism wasn't only a southern phenomenon. It had deep roots in American political culture going back to the Revolution, and during World War I, it was prevalent in the labor movement, the Socialist Party, and among leftwing progressives like Jane Addams, all of whom put their own spin on this complex of ideas. Midwesterners also believed in it, represented by Robert La Follette and William Jennings Bryan. Still, the antimilitarist ideology was especially intense among rural southerners. Its political base in Washington lay chiefly with southerners including congressional leaders like Claude Kitchin of North Carolina and James Hay of Virginia. And finally, it was part of Woodrow Wilson's outlook, although not to the same degree as it was for someone like Kitchin. But Wilson definitely shared aspects of it.

What impact did this antimilitarist outlook have on America's involvement in the war? First, it's one reason why Wilson was slow to embrace defense increases after the war started. Republicans started to push for what they called "preparedness" again in late 1914, and Wilson resisted it. He made no effort to increase America's armed forces until after the *Lusitania* was sunk in spring 1915, and even then, he really didn't get the ball rolling on it until late 1915, and legislation wasn't introduced until early 1916. Secondly, antimilitarist ideology actually shaped the defense program that was enacted in 1916. There was no universal military training component to it, chiefly because James Hay of Virginia successfully blocked it in the House of Representatives. The administration had proposed a four-hundred-thousand-man force under federal control, but that was basically a nonstarter in the House of Representatives and was blocked by Hay and his committee considering the legislation. Instead the Wilson administration strengthened federal control over the National Guard as a compromise measure.[2] Third, antimilitarists led the successful effort in Congress to pay for the defense program with the first really progressive tax system the United States had ever had. This measure reflected their determination to prevent plutocrats and reactionaries from using preparedness to enrich themselves while it impoverished farmers and workers.[3]

The antimilitarist outlook was also a key reason for the antiwar sentiment that existed in Congress and in the country in 1917 and that persisted after America's entry into the war. On that point, it's really difficult to judge exactly how strong antiwar feeling was in the country in April 1917. The actual vote for war was very lopsided, with fifty representatives in the House and six senators voting against it. But on other votes prior to the war declaration, my own best guess is roughly about a third of the House of Representatives would have opposed the war and went along with it basically in order to support Wilson or out of a feeling of national unity. And laying behind that, I think, is this antimilitarist outlook. After war was declared, the antimilitarist perspective began to focus on conscription. The draft was especially unpopular in the South, and it provoked widespread evasion and resistance. The existence of that dissent, of the resistance to the draft and this percolating antiwar sentiment under the surface, in turn led the Wilson administration to pursue a policy of intense repression at home. As many of you probably know, one of the worst periods for civil rights and liberties in the United States was between 1917 and 1919.[4]

Finally, I'd argue that the ideology of antimilitarism was part of the logic behind Wilson's League of Nations proposal. Wilson thought that a collective security system would prevent arms races. Arms control was always part of any League of Nations proposal that Wilson made. He thought collective security would prevent arms races in future wars that he feared could militarize the United States and force the country into building a large-scale defense establishment that would threaten its freedoms at home. So the way I see it, antimilitarism was not just a southern way of thinking, but its intensity in the South and the way that it was represented by southern political leaders in Washington, DC, had a massive impact on how the United States viewed the war and how it responded to it. And certainly through Wilson, it had a big impact on the goals that the war was fought for, namely, the league.

JENNIFER KEENE: I'm going to pick up on several of these themes in terms of thinking about mobilizing manpower. Once the war was actually declared, a country that had not made great preparations to fight suddenly had to raise an army that would number in the millions, something that it had not done before. America chose a new path for how to do this by immediately enacting the Selective Service Act, thus depending on conscription as the major vehicle for raising troops in the US Army. Seventy-two percent of the men who served in the US Army during the First World War were actually drafted.

In the beginning, there was a period where people could still volunteer, but that volunteering did not go well in the South. As Ross already noted, even when the Selective Service system was put into place, there were high rates of draft evasion nationwide. It's an astronomical number. Eleven percent of draft-eligible men were considered to either have purposefully or perhaps unintentionally evaded the draft and one-third of that figure comes from the South, so we can see the region's antiwar, antimilitaristic ideology having a concrete impact. But I think it's important not to describe that draft evasion figure solely as a result of ideological principle. We need to consider how the draft functioned and also some policy decisions that the military made early on.

Selective Service operated by giving states quotas that they had to fill, but it was up to local boards to actually produce those men. White elites dominated local boards, which would gather to conduct the draft. They interviewed men, examined them, and ultimately adjudicated exemptions. And throughout this whole process, officials tried to learn lessons from past drafts, especially those of the Civil War, where things had not gone well.

The federal government ultimately decided to have two national registration days, one in 1917 and one in 1918. Every draft-eligible man—in 1917 between the ages of twenty-one and thirty and by 1918 between eighteen and forty-five—had to report on the same day to register for the draft. Communities throughout the nation planned great celebrations to honor these men as they registered, and they then subsequently received notices about when they were supposed to show up for their physical exam. Men also received cards about how to apply for an exemption. When you think about the system and you're sitting in Washington, DC, or New York City, this sounds like a great plan. Those places had mail delivery, good communication, transportation infrastructure, and comparatively high literacy rates. It was relatively easy for people to get to the appropriate places to register.

When you take all of this and you put it into southern rural communities, you see that right away things started to break down. You had people dispersed across the region, literacy rates were very low in certain areas, and even mail delivery was irregular. In fact, especially in places with high concentrations of sharecroppers, landowners received the mail of their laborers and might open and read it. This could turn sinister when white planters purposefully withheld draft notifications meant for their African American sharecroppers in part to protect their labor force—like the Great Migration, the draft threatened a negative impact on the southern economy—but also because receiving a second notice made the recipients delinquent. Then the planter could turn their workers in as delinquents and collect a fifty-dollar reward.

Giving local elites control over the draft operation actually reinforced the attitude that planter elites already had—that they owned their black workforce. The process facilitated planters making decisions for these workers about when to inform them of their draft obligation and when it was time to actually turn them over to the authorities, or maybe never tell black men that their draft notices had come and instead privately secure exemptions with local draft boards.

But there were other ways for individuals to easily evade the draft because as I just told you the first requirement for draft eligibility was age. Many people born in rural areas did not have any government issued ID attesting to how old they were. People didn't have birth certificates, they didn't have driver's licenses, they often didn't even have school records. There was nothing to demonstrate that they were twenty-one. Your poverty might put you at the margins of this new bureaucracy, one that was coming into shape to categorize you by issuing new forms of identification to help the state count its manpower resources. Poor people could exist in the shadows of the emerging system because there was no way if someone came and said, "I think you're twenty-three," for them to prove it. In this way poor men who wanted to evade the draft, both white and black, could slip through the system.

Operation of the draft was predicated upon the idea that the local bureaucratic infrastructure could support the process. In the South, this bureaucracy just didn't exist in some places, so there could be logistical as well as antimilitaristic reasons for the high incidence of draft evasion in that region.

But many men didn't evade the draft. There were certainly plenty of people who, as Mike suggested, were enthusiastic about the war, who were interested in going. I don't want to at all give the impression that the South did not draft men and men did not go. The draft process marked the first time that the country was creating a national army of citizen soldiers, and many southerners eagerly joined that effort. In fact, the war was seen as an opportunity to put the Civil War to rest and symbolically foster reconciliation between the North and South. The notion of the military as a regional melting pot, mixing men from all walks of life to fight this campaign together, refashioned sectional loyalties into national ones.

I'll just point to a few ways in which we can see this process unfolding. The first national registration day, on June 5, 1917, included a parade in Washington, DC, viewed by Wilson, all of his cabinet, and many senators and congressmen. As the men marching to register for this draft went by, they were accompanied by Confederate and Union veterans. The Union veterans carried the American flag, and the Confederate veterans carried the stars and bars, and everybody welcomed this as perfectly appropriate.

The second really important way to see how the war facilitated reconciliation is to look at the names of the camps that were created. There were sixteen National Army camps and sixteen National Guard camps built to house all these men, and they were named after both Union and Confederate generals. This was not an accident; it was an intentional attempt to use this war to put sectional differences in the past. Affixing the names of Confederate war heroes to federal army installations demonstrated that the South was a distinct region whose concerns needed to be addressed in order for reconciliation to occur. This recognition reconstructed "southern identity" as patriotic and loyal, rather than traitorous.

Racial politics offers another example of the South's influence on federal wartime policy.[5] The military made an early decision to assign the majority of African Americans to noncombatant roles. The South pushed hard for this policy, claiming that a race war would result at home if the majority of black veterans received training in firearms. While this policy is probably unsurprising, it did have serious ramifications for poor white southern men because the first priority in mobilization was to draft combatants, get them into the training camps, train them, and transport them to France. Combatants needed a lengthier period of training, so the real drafting of African American troops did not start in earnest until March 1918. This means that in southern states that got a state quota based on population, the majority of men who went to fight and the majority of men who were called in those first draft calls were poor white men. They would be disproportionately drafted in the beginning, and then, officials very intentionally tried to make up for that discrepancy in 1918 by overdrafting African American soldiers. When you shake it all out, it turns out that African American men ended up being overdrafted in terms of their proportion of the population. Nonetheless, throughout the South in 1917, there was a prevalent view that communities were being drained of their white men, with black men left behind. This created an intense racial dialogue about who was fighting and who was not. Even though it was at the South's insistence that African Americans weren't being drafted as combatants, we see public hysteria growing over the notion that drafting white men in droves placed white women in danger of sexual assault from the black men left behind. There are many reasons for the spike in racial violence during the war, and this fear is one of them.

I emphasize "poor" white men to draw our attention to how the southern cotton economy was organized. If you were a planter who grew cotton, an essential war commodity, your son could get an exemption. But if you were a poor white farmer who was subsistence farming, your labor was not contributing in any way to the larger cause. You were not in an exempt occupational category and even being married was unlikely to get you an exemption because the sad fact was that both poor white and African American men could often make more money by serving as a private in the military than they could make in a month at home. Therefore they couldn't even argue that their dependents would suffer if they went into the military.

So far, I've addressed the big picture, but in conclusion, I wanted to tell the more personal story of a soldier, Edwin Frick of Dallas, Texas, who served in the Thirty-Sixth Division. Chapman University houses the Center for American War Letters, which contains wonderful letter collections that have been donated to us over the last few years. My students transcribed Frick's collection of letters last year. How did his roots in the South affect the way that he experienced the military and the way that he experienced going to France? He has a kind of tragic story because he trained in the artillery, got to France, and almost immediately started having health problems. He had trench foot, he had influenza, he was in and out of the hospital at least three times. He made it to February 1919, and his last letter home said, "Can't wait to see you." The next letter his parents receive was from the hospital notifying them that he had died from flu-related complications. This was three months after the war ended. There is nothing distinctively southern about any of these aspects of his wartime service. But in his letters, you can readily see that he retained and continually asserted— even though he was in this national army and he was overseas—his Texan identity.

His pride in the wartime accomplishments of Texans are impossible to ignore. Almost every letter home, he talked about how well Texans were doing, and he romanticized life in Dallas. In each subsequent letter he loved Dallas more, and the city became ever more desirable the longer that he was gone.

But the most distinctive signifier of Edwin's "southernness" was his commitment to the color line. He was sent to the hospital for trench foot and influenza, and when he wrote to his parents about these experiences, he talked about two things—his physical problems and the fights that he had with hospital administrators over integrated wards or mess halls— surprisingly common occurrences in army hospitals. I'll let Edwin explain what it meant to be white and from the South during the war: "He gave me a bed between two negroes, and after a flat refusal he moved me. He said, 'You sure are particular.' I said, 'Yes I am. I am from Texas.' In the mess hall, I had the same trouble. One sat next to me. I moved. One man who was in charge asked me where I was going. I told him, 'To another table.' He said, 'You might as well get used to them now as later.' I replied, 'No. No I wouldn't, as I come from where there is a distinction.'"

AUDIENCE: Jennifer, this ties into where you ended but also to your earlier point about reconciliation. I'm curious if you have any sense of where the African American community was on that point because, as we know, reconciliation was primarily built on the backs of African Americans who were excluded from that vision. Do you have a sense of how the black community felt?

KEENE: This was absolutely a contested idea in the African American community and the African American press. For example, we can see opposition to reconciliation in reactions to the army's singing program. The army had an official songbook and hoped that by learning the same songs, soldiers would learn to love America. You have patriotic hymns, but you also have songs like "Dixie." And the black press objected, arguing that it was wrong to try to unify by singing these southern songs that are glorifying slavery, that are glorifying the Confederacy. But they stayed in the book. This is the same moment as *Birth of a Nation*, which rehabilitated the Klan as the savior of white womanhood and promoted the notion that the North and South could unify around the rubric of white supremacy. We are talking about the South here, but let's not forget that some of the worst instances of wartime racial rioting and violence against African Americans occurred in the North, so the notion of basing reconciliation on white supremacy was not as contested as we might have wished looking back.

AUDIENCE: I wanted to ask at the beginning of the conference, not just to the panel but to the experts in the room on southern history— how should we be thinking of the definition of "the South," what is "the South," and are there different opinions when it comes to the answer to that question?

KENNEDY: I'm a political historian mostly, I do US foreign policy, so when I was confronted with the question, the way I looked at it was, "Where's the South's political power?" Obviously, there's Wilson, the administration was full of southerners, and key committees of Congress were very much southern dominated. The Democratic Party controlled both houses, and the South was the base of the Democratic Party. Obviously, that's just one element of the South, but it's one angle and I think it's surprisingly often forgotten that that was the case in Washington during the war, the prevalence and dominance of southerners in key policy-making positions. So that's just one angle on it, but I think it's an important one.

NEIBERG: One thing I'm going to add to that: in 1916, when Charles Evans Hughes was running for president, his campaign sort of defined the South as the states they weren't going to be able to compete in at all. So it was in the former Confederate states that he said, "Don't even bother." These are the southern states they knew were reliably Democratic, and the two things meant something similar to Hughes's people—the Democratic Party was the South plus the urban machines in the North. So in the North they could compete, in the South they couldn't.

KENNEDY: One thing to add is that during the war when Wilson was doing his economic mobilization and they were controlling the agricultural sector of the economy and they were setting wheat prices and cotton prices, the wheat price was set at a price that many midwesterners considered to be too low. And the cotton price, on the other hand, was allowed to rise, and midwesterners resented that terribly. The Republicans used that, especially in the 1918 congressional elections. They said, "This is regionalism. This is a southern president favoring his region over everybody else." The Republicans whipped that up in 1918 to kind of "wave the bloody flag" again.[6]

AUDIENCE: The question on how we define the South got me thinking about how we define the Great War. A hundred years ago, the United States was mobilizing in the Great War. At the same time, the United States was occupying Haiti, the United States was occupying the Dominican Republic, or areas of it. Now, where do you put those two rather prolonged conflicts in the narrative of the Great War?

NEIBERG: So there are some things that link. One is, the Americans deeply suspected that the Germans were messing around with the Mexican Civil War, which we now know they were. Pancho Villa himself bragged that the Germans had funded his raid into New Mexico, and the Panama Canal opened in 1914 so there were concerns about Caribbean security. The United States bought the Danish Virgin Islands and made them the US Virgin Islands in 1916, and the reason was they were afraid that Germany would either invade Denmark or threaten to invade Denmark, take the Virgin Islands, and then build a naval base there. This was the first time the United States thought seriously about using Puerto Rico as a method of hemispheric defense. So yes, these things were all connected in the minds of a lot of Americans, and not just in Washington but nationwide. Germany had done this in Ireland in trying to break southern Ireland away from the United Kingdom, the British did this in the Arab Revolt, so there's nothing particularly unusual in another state, in this case Germany, trying to make trouble on a national border like they were trying to do in Mexico. So in a certain sense yes, these things are all connected and things like the Virgin Islands are an example of how to deal with that. Haiti didn't begin this way, but the old political motto "never let a good crisis go to waste," suggests that if you were already there and you were worried about Caribbean security, it was one less incentive to leave.

AUDIENCE: I've got two questions, one unfairly narrow, the other unfairly broad. I teach Mississippi history and know that James Vardaman was one of the six senators who voted against the war. I'm wondering if you know much about his rationale and if it was shared by other people in the Mississippi delegation. The broader question is for Ross: you mentioned that antimilitarism in the rural South goes back to populism and age-old fears about standing armies, but I think it's kind of interesting because we think of the South—and I focus on post-1945—the South today is one of the most promilitary regions in the country, supporting high military budgets and serving as the site of a disproportionate number of military bases. Is that therefore a shift that happened because of World War II and the Cold War?

KENNEDY: Antimilitarism didn't mean antimilitary per se; it was that southerners didn't like the kind of professional standing armies controlled by Washington, DC, or controlled by the executive branch and the president. But local militias, they were all for that. So the sort of voluntaristic citizen-soldier type, that image, was OK and consistent with democracy and with the republic. This suspicion of federally controlled conscripted or professional forces diminished over the course of the early-mid-twentieth century for a variety of reasons. In part it happened because proponents of larger federal forces argued that universal military service brought men of different backgrounds together and so was consistent with fostering democratic citizenship. This idea of the regular army as democratic melting pot was especially spurred on by World War II.

On Vardaman, he and Kitchin and others in Congress echoed William Jennings Bryan and his analysis of the war's relationship to US security, namely that it didn't have one. They didn't see it as necessary to get involved in the war. It was a distraction, poor people were going to bear the burden of fighting it, it was just going to enrich Wall Street, and, more basically, it shouldn't matter to US safety who won the war in Europe. Those were the fundamental reasons why they opposed it.

ANDREW HUEBNER: If I can just add one thing to that, Vardaman and other senators voting against the war resolution said they had seen orphans and limbless veterans in the Civil War. Why would they do that again to enrich munitions makers in the Northeast?

AUDIENCE: When preparedness began, were southerners campaigning to have military installations built in their states? When they were actually building these installations, were they trying to prevent the health and supply issues that plagued southern military installations in the South during the Spanish-American War, or were they making it up as they went?

KEENE: Well, probably yes to all those things. There's certainly an amount of lobbying that went on in terms of people believing that bringing a national encampment to your area was going to be a source of jobs. People had to supply these camps, and so there was certainly an economic incentive to bringing them. What's interesting is that the majority of camps were located in the South, and part of the reason was that officials ironically believed that it would be a more temperate climate—a climate more conducive to constructing the camps faster and getting by with tents while construction was underway. But the winter of 1918 was a record cold winter in the South, creating great hardship for the soldiers in the camps. Army officials were certainly trying hard to construct them in a way that would eliminate disease—a lot of open air and ventilation. But the other irony is that the influenza epidemic, which they couldn't control at all, also occurred in 1918.

Military camp construction became a political process, generating debates over where they were located, how they were constructed, who supplied them. But not everybody saw a military installation in their neighborhood as a positive development. Many people worried that soldiers would bring a lot of undesirable elements into the community. And then you know, soldiers like to gamble, they like to find women, they like to drink, and all of these activities became undesirable things that soldiers could bring to your community if they were not held in check. I didn't mention this before, but officials gave a tremendous amount of thought about how to distribute African American soldiers throughout these encampments. There was a lot of discussion throughout the South about making sure that all these camps had a white majority to offer a clear, visible demonstration of African Americans' subjugation. These discussions were dominated by claims that large concentrations of black soldiers would likely get out of hand—and this policy, by the way, hampered the training of the Ninety-Second Division, a black combatant division whose units were trained separately in the United States. It never trained together until the men got to France. It's an interesting conversation that was going on as basically small cities were being created across the United States.

NEIBERG: Kitchin had no problem taking money. As much as he was opposed to preparedness, if that money was coming to North Carolina, he had no problem at all. The other thing I would just add is that my institution, the Army War College, was created because officials believed that the Spanish-American War process had gone so unbelievably badly. What they were trying to avoid was a repeat of what they saw as a disastrous war effort, and it gets back to some of the stuff that we've been talking about.

The debate was who was going to control this? So the reformers, the progressives in the army, the secretary of war who resigned, William Lindley Garrison, believed that if you put this in the hands of locals, it was just going to get screwed up the way it was screwed up the last time, that it had to be nationalized. And then folks like Kitchin, Vardaman, and others argued that no, what the federal government ought to do was give us the resources and then let us do it, which as Ross pointed out in the 1916 National Defense Act kept the National Guard in place but made it subject to federal standards and federal regulations. So you get this weird hybrid mix, that the United States still has, that is the product of the 1916 National Defense Act. The question wasn't, "Do you want to build a new infrastructure?" Everybody agreed you had to do that. The question was, "Who's going to control it and who's going to create it?" So part of the reason for putting these things in the South was to get the votes of folks like Kitchin.

AUDIENCE: Anyone who knows anything about James Vardaman knows he was a rabid racist as well. Can we think about war mobilization through the lens of white supremacy, as a mobilization of ideas that perhaps speaks to the heightened significance of the South within the larger war mobilization process?

NEIBERG: I would mention, just because Vardaman's involved in all of this, in the proposal to redo the national army, William Lindley Garrison and the DC officials wanted no language on segregation, no language on race at all. The idea that Garrison had was that the army that would be created in 1916 would eventually become a completely integrated army. That's the reason Vardaman came out opposed to the bill. It's the only reason, and Representative Hay in Virginia, same thing. If this was what the federal government had in mind, it was not even open for negotiation. And this was one of the reasons that William Lindley Garrison resigned, because of this conflict over what to do about the language of segregation in what he called the Continental Army Plan. So I would 100 percent agree, this language was in there; the ideas were in there that they were not willing even to challenge the idea of segregation even if the national military establishment believed that it was essential for fighting the war and getting the nation prepared. It's absolutely in those ideas.

KEENE: White supremacy was ideologically accepted nationwide, not just in the South. This was not going to be another Civil War in the sense of ending with an expansion of civil rights for African Americans. The shared ideology of white supremacy was reflected in the way that the military was organized. Over the course of the war, officials increasingly disparaged African Americans' ability to serve in combatant units. At the beginning of the war, plenty of army officers said, "It's clear that African American soldiers can fight. Now maybe they can't lead, but they definitely can fight." But, in a concession to the South, the military officially decided to put the majority of black soldiers in noncombatant units. Pretty soon, to justify that decision, army reports started regularly claiming that black soldiers were racially unfit to fight in an industrialized war. The wartime military created institutional structures with an accompanying racialized ideology that reinforced segregation and racial discrimination, making white supremacy within the military harder to change and harder to fight.

NEIBERG: And Vardaman, if I remember correctly and I think I have it in the book, when he spoke out against the Continental Army Plan, he didn't say, "This is a violation of American traditions." He said, "This is a violation of Democratic traditions," and he meant the Democratic Party, not democracy. I didn't do this in the book, but I was going to look at this moment as the beginning of the fracturing of the Democratic Party between its southern white branch and its northern urban branch. This was where it began to break, and it started with Vardaman and Kitchin and their opposition to any idea that the national emergency of the war was going to create this kind of change at home.

KENNEDY: The phrase you used, "mobilization of ideas," really captures the whole way Wilson pitched the war. He went for the highest, most idealistic phrasing he could come up with: "make the world safe for democracy," fight to vindicate self-government, and so on. But self-government for whom? It's self-government for specific white countries, places like Belgium were what he was talking about. He was not talking about ending imperialism. He was not talking about decolonization. Wilson very much had a color hierarchy in his conception of international relations just as much as he did at home. But in pitching the war that way, which in his mind was a way to mobilize the public to support it, it led people to take his words seriously. And so they said, "Well yeah, we should have freedom. Why is there imperialism in Asia and Africa? Why are African Americans treated as second-class citizens?" So it ended up sparking resistance to Western imperialism in colonized nations and contributed to rising African American demands for civil rights at home—unintended consequences from Wilson's point of view.

AUDIENCE: If the South is the Bible Belt, what role do religion and churches play in the debate over American involvement in the war and also in mobilization?

NEIBERG: In *The Path to War*, I cite quite a few southern religious leaders, especially a group out of Nashville that was close to William Howard Taft's secretary of war, who was from Nashville. What a lot of them were saying from 1914 to 1917, if there was a consensus message, was that if there was a terrible war going on in Europe, if the United States believed that this war was an immoral act, if the United States believed that people were suffering, but the main result for the United States was that our economy would grow and we would get rich, then we needed to ask ourselves serious questions about who we are as a people. So it was out of the churches—and it was not just the South, it was in the North too—where there was a debate over whether the United States should remain neutral. And I think it was actually the church people who separated from the position of neutrality earliest. Then the reaction was, well what was it that we ought to do? And there were two different strands. There was the strand of, we ought to help everybody who's suffering no matter where they are, regardless of their politics. And then there was the strand that I think was nationwide, but it was strong in this group in Nashville whose records I looked at, which was that the Allies were the right side. There was a right and there was a wrong, and the United States standing aside in a war of right and wrong did not reflect well on what we thought we were as a nation. So I wouldn't say that that was a unanimous opinion of course, but it was a consensus view of many of the southern religious leaders.

KEENE: I think the session later with Jonathan Ebel will address this question. The only thing I would add here concerns the difficulties in the South for people who wanted to declare conscientious objector status based on their religious beliefs. Men who belonged to small poor religious sects that weren't recognized as legitimate religious organizations by the government had a very difficult path to follow in terms of actually using religious principles as a justification for not serving in the military. In that sense I think that you can see how the structure of the Selective Service system privileged the way religious life was organized in urban areas as opposed to the practice of rural locally based religious organizations throughout the South.

AUDIENCE: I know we talked about reconciliation between the North and South, but how did southerners serving in the military react to training and fighting alongside people from the North? I know in the Forty-Second Division you had the 167th Alabama Infantry Regiment fighting alongside the 168th Iowa Infantry.

KEENE: If you were poor or working class, which most Americans were, you had probably never traveled beyond a forty- or fifty-mile radius from where you were born. These men did not ever anticipate traveling across the country, seeing New York City, getting on a boat, going to Europe. Military service allowed you to see parts of America you never thought you would see, meet people from different regions you never thought you would meet. This was a typical part of every American soldier's experience during the war. I wouldn't say that southerners were unique in the novelty of visiting new places, seeing different customs, and coming into contact with people from different states or countries.

One of every five soldiers in the US Army in the First World War was foreign born, so it was very likely that you were going to come into contact with people who were born in Italy, who were born in Russia, who were born in France. You certainly see plenty of commentary about meeting Jews for the first time, meeting Catholics for the first time, meeting somebody from New York City for the first time. But I wouldn't want to say that this is a uniquely southern experience. I think that this is a universal aspect of serving in a wartime military that used Selective Service to create a *national* army with a sort of melting-pot quality to it. I don't think in earlier militaries they were trying to erase regional identities or trying to create a sense of "we are all Americans and this is what unifies us." But going back to singing—that was just one example of how the army tried to inculcate recruits with similar concepts of what it meant to be American. I always find it so interesting that people were brought into the military and had to be taught the national anthem. They had to be taught the meaning of American iconography. There was a lot of emphasis on what the flag means, what the Statue of Liberty means, what the eagle means. People had to be taught these things. They were teaching people how to understand the symbols and values associated with Americanness. And that was happening nationwide. In a sense, the project of creating a national army involved erasing "foreignness," "southernness," and "northernness"—trying to unify around the identity of "Americans All." Of course, that was the ambition, but not necessarily what happened—as I noted earlier Edwin Frick remained a Texan until the day he died.

HUEBNER: One of the people I wrote about in *Love and Death in the Great War* was from Selma, Alabama, a white southerner. He came here to UA and ended up enlisting and going to New York before leaving for Europe. He was in the Eighty-Second Division, known as the "All Americans" because it drew from so many different regions. He had strong and not always positive opinions about people from other parts of the country.

Notes

1. For details, see Ross A. Kennedy, *The Will to Believe: Woodrow Wilson, World War I, and America's Strategy for Peace and Security* (Kent, OH: Kent State University Press, 2009), 1–24.

2. On the legislative battle over preparedness, see Arthur S. Link, *Wilson: The Struggle for Neutrality, 1914–1915* (Princeton, NJ: Princeton University Press, 1960), 592–93; Link, *Wilson: Confusions and Crises, 1915–1916* (Princeton, NJ: Princeton University Press, 1964), 15–54, 321–38.

3. On the tax bill, see Link, *Wilson: Confusions and Crises*, 339–41; and Thomas J. Knock, *To End All Wars: Woodrow Wilson and the Quest for a New World Order* (New York: Oxford University Press, 1992), 89–90.

4. See Jeanette Keith, *Rich Man's War, Poor Man's Fight: Race, Class, and Power in the Rural South during the First World War* (Chapel Hill: University of North Carolina Press, 2004); and Christopher Capozzola, *Uncle Sam Wants You: World War I and the Making of the Modern American Citizen* (New York: Oxford University Press, 2008).

5. See Jennifer D. Keene, *Doughboys, The Great War, and the Remaking of America* (Baltimore: Johns Hopkins University Press, 2001).

6. On the 1918 election, see David Burner, *The Politics of Provincialism: The Democratic Party in Transition, 1918–1932* (Cambridge, MA: Harvard University Press, 1986), 10–73; and David Sarasohn, *The Party of Reform: Democrats in the Progressive Era* (Jackson: University Press of Mississippi, 1989), 193–237.

2

Fighting the Great War Over Here

Martin T. Olliff, Nancy K. Bristow, and Jessica L. Adler

When America formally entered the First World War in 1917, no one really knew what the long-term consequences would be for southern society. Marty Olliff, Nancy Bristow, and Jessica Adler turned our attention to how the war directly affected the South as a region and what role it played in the daily lives of southerners. Much of the conversation centered on how dramatic shifts in the regional economy and healthcare system raised profound questions of change and continuity in race relations. Olliff, in his talk on the growth of military bases in Alabama, wryly observed that the South's white leaders loved the influx of outside dollars but feared outside ideas, especially ones that challenged segregation. Bristow and Adler showed how white southerners attempted to preserve racial power while struggling to build a healthcare system able to cope with the flu pandemic and care for returning veterans. On this matter, Adler offered an important perspective on how black southerners fought the color line being built into the new Veterans Administration. Audience members moved discussion to the feelings of veterans themselves about the Veterans Administration, the ways the flu influenced popular ideas of postwar memorialization, and the quality of medical care received by black veterans and citizens.

MARTY OLLIFF: When looking for a dissertation topic in the 1990s, my friend Gordon Harvey, now chair of the history department at Jacksonville State University, asked, "Why are there so many military bases in Alabama?" While Gordon did not pursue that I'd like to talk about it now. Although this is a new area of research for me, I've come to realize the answer is that Alabama wants outside money but doesn't want outside ideas. Alabama was happy to have multiple military bases and infrastructure projects established by the federal government during World War I. It welcomed them. It reached out to the federal government and said "bring 'em on!" At the same time, Alabama resisted anything that threatened what we have come to call "the southern way of life." I believe Alabama's willingness to accept federally funded projects might have been enhanced by the army's and Wilson administration's known promotion of Jim Crow segregation.[1] In the time we have today, I hope to sketch the contours of the story that, with luck, other scholars and I will be able to track more fully in the future.

Two of the thirty-two major World War I training camps in the United States were here in Alabama: Camp Sheridan, named for Phil Sheridan, and Camp McClellan, which later became Fort McClellan, named for . . . some other Union general, who remembers?[2] But let me tell you about how much Montgomery wanted Camp Sheridan. It wanted Camp Sheridan so much that it worked behind the scenes and made direct overtures to Gen. Leonard Wood, commanding officer of the Southeastern Department of the US Army who was responsible for siting many of these camps.[3] Rep. Stanley H. Dent from Alabama's Second Congressional District (which included Montgomery) and chairman of the House committee on military affairs, reached out both to the War Department and to General Wood to get Camp Sheridan away from other states and to get it away from Birmingham and Mobile.[4] On June 25, 1917, Montgomery mayor W. T. Robertson offered General Wood a contract between the city and the US government that included two thousand acres of land rent free just north of town. The city promised to lay a water main that could handle two million gallons per day for a cost of ten cents per thousand gallons, which was substantially lower than what water cost in town. City leaders also promised to erect an electricity grid to supply two hundred kilowatts per day at three cents per kilowatt, again, very low rates. Finally, the city was to furnish up to twenty-five million board feet of lumber to construct the camp at nineteen dollars per one-thousand board feet. Wood signed this contract on June 25.[5]

The cost to build this camp in the first year was $1.5 million, and the contract went to Algernon Blair Company, which was a local Montgomery construction outfit.[6] So $1.5 million, big deal, right? In 2016 dollars, that's $57.4 million. Now, $57.4 million goes a long way to reversing the sting of having that camp named for a Union general. And believe me, there was a lot of reaction to that in Montgomery. The Lost Cause wasn't nearly as lost then as it later became. The monthly payroll—and this goes a long way also to salving that sting too—was $1.38 million. That's $52.8 million in 2016. Also, the anticipated annual boom to the local Montgomery economy of having 27,000 to 30,000 soldiers in a town of 40,000 was $16.6 million (in 1917), which was $635 million dollars in 2016, per year into the local economy.[7] I'll settle for half of that in cash right now.

Montgomery also got Taylor Field, which trained 139 pilots and had 200 airplanes, 11 miles southeast of town, and the federal government got 800 acres of land for $4,000 a year. Taylor Field was paired with Repair Depot No. 3, situated on the former site of the Wright Brothers' flight school along the railroad tracks 2 miles west of downtown Montgomery. Repair Depot No. 3 served not only Taylor Field, but also air service stations throughout the Southeast. The army never completely deactivated the depot, and in 1922, it became what is now Maxwell Air Force Base.[8] Montgomery was very much involved in seeking Taylor Field and Repair Depot No. 3 as well as Camp Sheridan.

The same thing happened near Anniston, in northwest Alabama. There, Camp McClellan grew from Camp Shipp that had served as a training camp and departure station for the US Army during the Spanish-American War. From Camp Shipp's four thousand acres, Camp McClellan expanded to 19,000 acres. It's 8 miles north of Anniston, and about 8 miles south of Jacksonville. The 1910 census reported the population of Anniston at 12,800 and the population of Jacksonville at 2,200. So the army brought in 27,000 people making 30 bucks a month and gave Anniston, like Montgomery, a pretty big boost to its economy. Camp McClellan hosted the 29th Infantry Division, which was similar in size to the 37th Division, those Ohio boys who trained at Camp Sheridan. It was difficult to find sufficient labor in a town that small so the first elements of the 29th had to help build the camp. They built about half of it, making about half of the money that the construction laborers were making. They were not happy. Like Camp Shipp had done two decades before, and like Camp Sheridan did in central Alabama, Camp McClellan had African American troops who trained there. The distance from Anniston to Camp McClellan, the short time the white 29th Division was there, and the fractious racial history between black troops and white residents during the Spanish-American War slowed fraternization between citizens and soldiers. But romances bloomed nonetheless, and some soldiers returned to marry locals after the war.[9]

In the northeast corner of the state, at Muscle Shoals on the Tennessee River, where today Joel Mize and Richard Sheridan are in charge of a historical marking, and possible restoration, project, Air Nitrates and Cyanamid built two plants to distill nitrates from the air, which was a German process perfected in 1913.[10] It required huge amounts of electricity so the federal government built the Wilson Dam there, which was of course not finished by the end of the war. The plants generated no nitrates by the end of the war, either, because we were only in the war for nineteen months. But the impact of the federal money invested in the entire Muscle Shoals

Project was tremendous as was its threat to the Jim Crow social system. To maintain racial segregation, infrastructural improvements like housing and public accommodations had to be made in pairs. Consequently, the Florence-Tuscumbia-Sheffield-Muscle Shoals area faced a real issue of what to do with the great migration of workers and their families who didn't go up North but came from countryside into town in order to work at these construction sites. Again, the war ended, and work ceased before the towns were able to come to a full accommodation with the influx of new arrivals.[11]

Mobile faced the same kind of economic and social disruption because the US Emergency Fleet Corporation expanded shipbuilding there dramatically. Of the five major shipbuilding companies that secured federal contracts in the Mobile area, only TCI (formerly Tennessee Coal and Iron Company), which was the Alabama arm of US Steel operating from Birmingham, got $20 million in federal funds to build housing for its workers as well as its docks. That's $765 million in 2016 dollars.[12] TCI created three different companies in order to build their shipyard, build their ships, and build the town of Chickasaw, which was where they housed their workers. They put in deep slips, they paved streets, they built craftsman style cottages, and many of these laborers that built this town ended up living there after the war when they moved from building ships to other local employment.[13] There were four other companies that operated near downtown Mobile, and really, my interest in these companies concerns the impact of bringing in so many people to work. What happened to Mobile? I don't have time today to go into that as much as I would like. Fortunately, Matthew Downs, a scholar at the University of Mobile, is looking at this right now.[14] The company called ADDSCO (Alabama Dry Dock and Shipbuilding Company) built a semi-independent community, according to John Sledge, at Pinto Island, which is just across the river from downtown Mobile. They had 4,000 workers, although Mike Thompson said there were 3,600, with a payroll of $500,000 monthly. Mobile Shipbuilding Company, which was the local affiliate of the Kelly Atkinson Company of Chicago, had $10 million in contracts and by 1918 was reported to have contracts for $12. I suspect that includes the $10 million, for 12 ships for $1 million each. Fred T. Ley Company of Springfield, Massachusetts, was one of only a handful of companies authorized to build concrete hull vessels. Its facility was either at Garrows Bend or McDuffie Island, just south of downtown. Ley had 4,000 workers with a payroll of $120,000 to $160,000 a month.[15] And then there's the Murrin Corporation; I have found no real information on that, and it's one subject that I want to explore further. So there were five corporations in or just north of Mobile pouring $5 million per year of what Mobilians called "ship money" into the city's economy by 1920 ($59.9 million in 2016 dollars).[16] How did Mobile handle this influx of money and the workers who came to earn it? Let me make an analogy: I like to drink water, but I don't like to drink it from a fire hose. Mobile drank from the fire hose. In other presentations in which I deal with the economic or with the social impacts of all of this money coming in, I call it an "embarrassment of riches." Neither the state of Alabama nor these localities had the infrastructure to take care of this tremendous influx of workers in particular. Prices skyrocketed, and communities suffered all the evils that we associate with boomtowns. Fortunately, other scholars are studying this, but it is an area that definitely needs even more research in the future.

NANCY BRISTOW: I want to start with a poem written by an army private, Josh Lee, in 1919. While his words may not be great literature, they turn our attention to a subject important for our discussions today. He wrote, "It stalked into camp when the day was damp / And chilly and cold. It crept by the guards / and murdered my pards / with a hand that was clammy and bony and bold. / And its breath was icy and moldy and dank, / And it killed so speedy / And gloatingly greedy / That it took away men from each company rank."[17] Private Lee was not describing the German army or their arsenal. He was talking, instead, about an entirely different enemy, Spanish influenza. I'm going to shift us away from the military aspects of the Great War with my remarks today but stay with what I think of as a very important chapter in that history, the influenza pandemic of 1918 and 1919. I'll start by telling you a little bit about this scourge. Then I'll talk a bit about both the American, and the distinctly southern, experiences of the pandemic. And finally I'll end by explaining why I think it is vital that this medical and social calamity be part of our conversation about the war.

So what was the Spanish influenza pandemic? What happened? This was perhaps the worst pandemic in human history, as four waves of influenza, starting in the spring of 1918 and followed by three subsequent waves, washed over the globe. The worst of these was the second wave, which struck in the fall of 1918. Over the course of these four waves a third of human beings around the globe were infected, some five hundred million people. Somewhere between fifty and one hundred million people died worldwide.[18]

Americans were used to the flu, which struck each year with regularity, sickening people, and even sometimes killing them, usually among the very young and the elderly. And yet because of its regular presence and its tendency only to sicken in most cases, influenza was also domesticated for

Americans. It had become something they expected and did not particularly fear.[19]

In 1918, though, Americans quickly recognized that what they faced was not the same flu to which they had grown accustomed. A number of features brought this new reality home. First, this influenza moved very fast. The second wave hit Boston on August 27 and had reached Birmingham by the end of September. It spread over the entire nation over the course of those four weeks.[20] Soon Americans also recognized that this flu was deadly for a new set of victims. The majority of influenza casualties, then as now, were among the young and the old, and while this iteration certainly attacked those groups, it also featured a spike among young adults, claiming almost half of its victims among people between the ages of twenty and forty.[21] Not only was this surprising, but it was also socially destabilizing, disrupting families when parents were stricken, businesses when owners and customers fell ill, urban governments when public servants missed work, and the medical profession as doctors and nurses also succumbed to the disease. The illnesses and deaths of people in the prime of their lives was a shock for a country, and a world, already rocked by the losses of World War One.[22]

This new influenza also struck with what observers noted was unprecedented ferocity, infecting 28 percent of Americans. The mortality rate, in turn, was perilously high, at 2.5 percent, 25 times the normal rate for influenza. In America, 675,000 died during the pandemic, 500,000 more than would normally die of influenza over a similar period.[23] Think about what that scale of death would mean, even today when our population is significantly larger. The fear, the disruption, the sense of loss is unimaginable.

The South's experience in this scale of loss was comparable to that of the nation as a whole. Virginia suffered 200,000 cases on a single day in October.[24] Nashville lost 875 of its citizens to the flu, Atlanta 829.[25] Over 54,000 people were made ill by influenza in New Orleans, and 3,489 of them died.[26] Alabama had 26,000 cases in a single week, and Birmingham lost 135 people also in just one week.[27]

The realization that this influenza was something new was reinforced by its horrible symptoms. Most of us have had the flu, and we know, in the best circumstances, that it is a miserable illness. This influenza was the disease at its worst, bringing terrible pain in the joints and muscles, prostration, and a fever high enough that many people would become delirious and eventually lose consciousness. For many, the lungs filled with liquid, and people were literally drowning in their own bodily fluids. Their extremities would turn blue or purple or even black, and they might have bloody liquid coming out of their ears, mouth, or nose.[28] As one person remarked of his own illness, "I didn't care if I died or not."[29] I include these graphic, and admittedly horrific, details because we need to try to imagine these circumstances, both for those who were ill and those who served as their caretakers. Imagine, for instance, the emotions of a mother taking care of a child, a spouse watching a spouse. Americans, and people worldwide, were dealing with overwhelming circumstances of disruption, fear, and loss.[30]

With this context in mind, I want to shift us to thinking about the "social experience" of the disease, what it was actually like for those who suffered through the pandemic. Though influenza was indiscriminate in its victims, those who were stricken and those who sought to care for them did not all experience the pandemic in the same ways. Their process through the illness was shaped not only by the virus but also by the social and cultural norms and practices of their communities. This was true across the country, suggesting in some ways the southern experience was typical. And yet, of course, the region also had its own particular dynamics that produced unique circumstances for some sufferers.

Most important to note was the southern healthcare system, which was, at the time, a segregated system. Prior to the pandemic, the costs of this dual system, separated by race, was both evident and high. African Americans had always been desperately underserved, and with the rise of segregation alongside the modernizing of the medical profession, the inequities certainly did not lessen. Despite the fight for quality health care waged by black communities, they nevertheless experienced inadequate numbers of hospitals, of trained doctors, of nurses employed in public services. Before the pandemic struck, several markers of medical inequity were evident. For instance, African Americans faced markedly higher death rates from tuberculosis, typhoid fever, whooping cough, and infant diarrheal illnesses and a life expectancy of 38.9 years, compared to the more robust 55.1 years among white Americans.[31]

When the pandemic struck, the inequities continued, making more desperate the circumstances of people of color as they found their access to quality healthcare blocked by the norms of a segregated society. The city of Birmingham established two emergency hospitals, a common practice during the pandemic, and placed them alternatively in the all-white Central High School and the all-black Colored Industrial High School, to insure the separation of the races.[32] It is not hard to picture that the quality of those spaces and the resources distributed to them were dramatically different. In Richmond, when the Red Cross established an emergency hospital, African Americans were initially served in the basement.[33]

And yet while segregation was the law in southern states, the practice was evident in some northern communities as well, suggesting that racial mistreatment was actually a national phenomenon. Philadelphia, for instance, did not create any emergency hospitals for African Americans. It was up to the black community itself to create those hospitals.[34] It is more accurate to say, then, that regions across the country practiced racial discrimination, that race shaped the social experience of the pandemic, even as its impact varied depending on local traditions of white supremacy.

Another important factor in the social experience of the pandemic was economic class, with poverty causing truly desperate circumstances for many. For those already immersed in poverty, the loss of a breadwinner might mean hunger, an appeal to interventionist social welfare organizations, homelessness, even the necessity of giving up children to an orphanage.[35] In poorer rural areas the suffering could be still worse. This was certainly true in Kentucky, where, according to the Red Cross, "every problem was accentuated."[36] Many in the state suffered from deep poverty and lacked any local public health program or the most basic sanitation. The Red Cross described the circumstances in Pineville, for instance, where they found a home with nine stricken with influenza—two parents and seven children—all in a single room, with no one to care for them. In the town, according to the report, "people were starving, and had no medicine, and no nourishment."[37] Again, the South represented perhaps a more exaggerated form of a nationwide phenomenon.

But what does all of this have to do with the war? In fact, the war and the pandemic were intricately, and intimately, connected. Most obviously, this catastrophe took place in the midst of the war. It wreaked havoc on the war effort in a multitude of ways—from sickening soldiers to affecting domestic production. Because these impacts are easy to understand, I want to turn our attention to other, sometimes more subtle, linkages. First, the pandemic's origins were clearly connected to the war. Scholars continue to argue about the geographic roots of the virus, with some placing it at a military base in northern France, others in China or in Southeast Asia. Scholars continue to disagree, but given the first wave's presence in the United States, the theory that it emerged at Camp Funston at Fort Riley, Kansas, here in the United States, in April 1918, continues to be prominent. No one disputes, in turn, that the war facilitated its spread, even as the encampments likely helped in its process of genetic mutation into its pandemic form.[38] Keep in mind, in turn, that the South had far and away the largest number of military camps in the United States. The perfect storm of the virus was created in a perfect moment called the war.

Another important linkage between the pandemic and World War One was the simple reality that the war made the suffering of Americans during the pandemic worse. As a result of the war, large numbers of doctors and nurses were serving in the military, making access to healthcare, which was already only provisional for many populations, still more difficult.[39] In turn, four million young men were away from home in the armed forces. As people endured influenza, families were often separated. For those in the training camps or serving in Europe, they sometimes suffered without the same kind of care—attentive nursing—that family members might have provided.[40]

A third connection, and one that I find particularly interesting, was the way public health leadership used the war to sell the intrusive public health policies the pandemic required such as the closure of schools, churches, and public amusements, the cancellation of public events, even quarantines and public masking. The US Public Health Service had very little power in 1918, but local community health boards sometimes wielded more. In order to convince the public to obey, though, they often relied on the war to motivate the citizenry. One particularly telling example was a poster from the public health service in Connecticut that pleaded, simply, "Help Fight the Grippe," a slang term for the flu, "Kaiser Wilhelm's Ally."[41] Public health leaders attempted to enlist the public in fighting the flu by suggesting that the war required a healthy population. Citizens were asked to go along with whatever the government demanded because fighting the flu was a patriotic contribution to the war.[42]

And this leads to the final connection I want to make between the war and the pandemic. The strategy of the public health leadership proved successful, at least in part, because the war became conflated with the pandemic in Americans' minds. The pandemic, in a sense, came to be understood as part of the war in popular culture. Let me explain what I mean. For some people the connection with the war was literal. Many Americans believed that influenza was actually a German plot, that the illness had been intentionally brought to the United States from Germany. Some believed, for instance, that Bayer's aspirin carried the flu.[43]

Not every American believed this conspiracy theory, of course, and yet this conflation between the two events proved strikingly common. Even today Americans tend to use martial language to talk about disease. We repeatedly talk about "fighting" a cold; we declare a "war" on cancer. Similarly, during the pandemic Americans routinely discussed influenza as the "enemy," seeing the disease as "the invisible foe," the pandemic an "army of deadly influenza germs," "as dangerous as poison gas shells"; Americans strategized about how to "fight Spanish influenza," to "combat the thing."[44] What was remarkable during the pandemic was how completely this kind of martial language took hold, to the point that Americans equated service in the pandemic to service in the war, not just figuratively but quite literally as well. Nurses' service was compared to service on the front in Europe.[45] The New York City Department of Health suggested that the deaths of its workers during the pandemic "ought to rank them with those heroes who have given their lives in France for country and civilization."[46] At the University of Virginia, students who died of influenza were listed in the yearbook as "war dead."[47]

In these appeals to war imagery we can see, perhaps, the desperate effort to make meaning out of the meaningless influenza deaths. The war, it seems, allowed Americans to associate their suffering with a virtuous and important cause, imbuing their losses with value. At a funeral at Camp Sherman, for instance, we can see this tactic being enacted as one speaker suggested of those who died of influenza, "It's sweet to die for one's country. These men are as true martyrs as those who have died in the trenches."[48] These men had been stricken by influenza and died in camp, but here, they became martyrs who had died for their country.

The pandemic was a terrible and seemingly meaningless event that shattered Americans' confidence in healthcare and what they thought was the new capacity of science to protect them. The deaths were tragic, and Americans struggled to make sense of what had happened, to find meaning in the horrific losses they endured. As they looked for meaning, they found it in the war. Later today we'll be talking about finding meaning in the war. I want to suggest that people found meaning in the pandemic by connecting it *to the war*.

I would add a caveat to close. While this rhetorical strategy of linking the fight against influenza to the war was broadly employed, suggesting it served some use in the public conversations, I suspect it had very little meaning for those who were actually suffering in the aftermath of the pandemic. Though the nation might attempt to blot out, or recast, the losses of the pandemic by associating them with the war, the memory and experience of those losses continued in the lives of those left behind.[49]

JESSICA ADLER: I want to pick up on a few of the themes that have been mentioned throughout the morning. First, the idea brought up by Jennifer Keene—this notion of reconciliation and what this moment in time meant for creating a sense of nationalism. I'm going to touch, too, on Marty's point—that the South likes to receive outside money but not outside ideas. I think that's something that probably relates to a lot of the work of people in this room. And I think it's a principle that shapes regional histories—certainly veterans' healthcare. And Nancy's point about the particular situation of the South at a moment in time when public health was in its infancy is something that you'll hear in my talk too—that helped to shape ideas about veterans' healthcare.

So the work I do focuses on the beginning of the veterans' health system. And I want to start by just talking to you about *what happened*. So, in 1917, when the United States declared war, there were zero so-called veterans' hospitals in the United States. By 1941, a federal agency called the Veterans' Administration [VA], which had been established in 1921 as the Veterans' Bureau, was overseeing institutionally based care for more than seventy-one thousand veterans throughout the United States. Eighteen thousand of those seventy-one thousand veterans were in the South. That same year, 1941, the VA was funding care at ninety-one facilities across the country and twenty-six of those facilities were in the South.[50] Part of the point of the book I just wrote is that the story of the beginning of this health system tells us important things about the history of health and medicine. It tells us important things about the way social policy and entitlements work in the United States, and it tells us important things about the history of veterans' benefits—that this was, in many ways, a turning point in a lot of those different areas of history.[51]

I have to admit that this conference encouraged me to think about this story in a totally different respect—from the perspective of what it means for the history of the South. And it seems to me that it takes on a different significance. I want to propose to you that it's important to consider this story in the larger context of the history of the South. Because—and agreeing with Jennifer—I think that it highlights a really important moment—a weaving together of a nation, especially in a bureaucratic sense. So, I want to give you two examples of how this health system influenced the South and one example of how southerners shaped the health system. And these are proposals—I hope that we can talk about them.

So, my first proposal is that one way that the establishment of this health system influenced the South was that it dramatically increased the presence of the federal government here. And this draws on some of the points that have been made about prewar federal investment in the region. Many in this room are probably aware that, even though there were zero veterans' hospitals in 1917, there were plenty of other supports in existence for veterans. You could think of them as belonging in two general categories: soldiers' homes and pensions. It's important to understand that the idea of hospital care, first in the military and then through the veterans' health system, is rooted on the premise that soldiers' homes and pensions both foster dependency on the government in ways that curative medical care would not. The hope was that this new generation of veterans would be rehabilitated: they would be cared for in—ideally—a military hospital and never need the government again. But once it became clear that that goal was elusive, the hope became that this new generation of veterans would receive care in veterans' hospitals that would exist temporarily. Some soldiers' homes had hospitals on their campuses, but they were widely viewed by WWI-era policy makers, and by WWI-era veterans, as antiquated institutions that offered subpar medical care, to say the very least—not scientific medicine. So we see a conscious creation of a different type of veterans' benefit.

It's really important to understand that, when it came to the two types of veterans' benefits that I just mentioned—soldiers' homes and pensions—there were two parallel systems of each in the United States in the post–Civil War years. Confederate veterans had access to *state*-sponsored pensions and *state*-sponsored soldiers' homes. Meanwhile, Union veterans had access to *federally* sponsored pensions and *federally* sponsored soldiers' homes.

What I propose is: the federal government's sponsorship of a veterans' health system after World War I was a tremendous change nationwide—a massive expansion in federal power. In other words, if you were in New York City, and you were getting care from the federal government, that was somewhat novel and unprecedented at this moment. After all, before World War I, access to medical services in freestanding veterans' hospitals was not part of the postwar benefits package.

But it was even *more* unprecedented in the South, and that was in part because this was basically a moment when veterans' benefits in that region—on a massive scale—became "federalized."[52] This new generation of veterans from this major conflict would turn not primarily to their *state* governments, which had the support of local elites and local fundraisers. Instead, their main source of support after this war was going to be the federal government—a new federal agency and a new federal health system. This was a distinct change in the relationship between southerners and their national government.

So, that's proposal number one: the advent of the veterans' health system represented a massive expansion of the role of the state across the board but even more so in the South. We see a heightened presence of the federal government and new ways that southern citizen-veterans related to that federal government.

My second proposal has to do with the ideas Nancy discussed and the expansion in access to medical care that these facilities represented. So I talked about the fact that twenty-six of the ninety-one facilities that the veterans' administration was funding by 1941 were in the South. As Nancy told you, historians of health and medicine see the southern case as distinctive in many respects. We know that some epidemic diseases were much more of a threat in southern states, in large part because of the disproportionate percentage of the population that was impoverished. Interestingly, southerners were not idle in the face of these challenges and you see plenty of activism on the ground level. Black intellectuals were on the forefront of recognizing the connection between socioeconomic status and health and of providing programs and services to increase the public health of southern communities by calling for economic and social supports. There are many writings, not only from W. E. B. Du Bois but others too, at black colleges and universities, discussing the fact that socioeconomic uplift leads to better health.[53] And you also see local white elites attempting to bring southern communities and new southern cities up to par with public health efforts that were ongoing already in the North.[54] So this is not something that southerners were oblivious to.

But public health is different from individualized medical care and what you see in the Progressive Era, 1880 to about 1910, is the beginning of the "golden age of hospitals"; around that time period, the number of hospitals in the United States tripled to 4,300.[55] That happened, in part, because there was a changing perception of what these institutions could do. Prior to the advent of the germ theory of disease, prior to the creation of new technologies like the x-ray machine—these things all happened at the end of the nineteenth century—hospitals had just been seen as dens of destitution, if you will. But by 1910, with new understandings of science and the way germs were transmitted, with population movements to cities and changing structures of medical practice, and with advanced technologies available, hospitals were seen as places that could actually benefit patients. So, that provides some context for why you see the rise of this idea at all—that hospitals should be created and relied upon.

But the South was somewhat of an outlier. By 1938, the *Report on Economic Conditions of the South* noted that there were far fewer doctors per capita in South Carolina than there were in California. And there were far fewer medical institutions like hospitals and clinics than there were in other parts of the country.[56]

These ideas regarding the state of health and medicine in the South relate to my second proposal that, while the creation of federally sponsored veterans' hospitals represented a major change all over the country, in this disproportionately impoverished and underserved part of the country, they represented a more dramatic change.

So, those are the two proposals about how the new veterans' health system influenced the South in the post–World War I years: it represented a federalization of veterans' benefits and a boon in terms of access to medical services.

My third proposal has to do with how southerners influenced the veterans' health system. In my view, they played a key role in making it both more and less egalitarian. We see that if we examine debates about how accessible the system would be to different parts of the veteran population. Southerners had the most to gain or lose from this system adopting or not adopting the tenets of Jim Crow. So, we have white segregationists working to make sure that the veterans' health system was differentially accessible, and segregated, to the fullest extent. And we have black southerners and some progressive white southerners very actively fighting against that.

I'll give you two examples. First, the white segregationist perspective. We have, after WWI, the creation of the major national veterans' organizations that still exist today, specifically, the American Legion and Disabled American Veterans [DAV]. These organizations are part of the story of the veterans' health system because they're the ones whose leaders worked with legislators to write the laws that led to the first veterans' hospitals—and that shaped veterans' benefits for the next century. In the archives of the American Legion, we find letters from, for example, black lawyers from Georgia saying, "We're trying to get our own chapter of the American Legion started here in Atlanta. Can we get a charter?" and the state leaders from the Georgia Legion replying that they won't grant the charter. And you also see letters from state legion offices in Georgia to the national office of the American Legion saying, "We're actually getting a lot of these letters, and we're not sure what to do because a lot of these black veterans want to be part of our group and we think that may really make our white members flee. And we don't want that to happen." And what you see in the minutes of the closed-door meetings of these very politically powerful organizations is that state leaders were, in many ways, gently fighting with the national leadership. National leaders were saying things like, "we understand that this is a particular southern situation, and you are particularly suited to deal with your own situation, but we have to answer this question about membership; our organization's constitution says that we represent all veterans." What you see, in the end, is that the ideology of white segregationist southerners was—at least in the early years of the legion—adopted. They argued,

"This is a state's rights issue; state chapters should govern the state-level rules." So, the American Legion and DAV, when they were first established, yielded to the concerns of their most devotedly segregationist leaders—disregarding the more progressive views of others—and limited membership rights for black veterans who were fighting for access.[57]

The reason I mention that example is because, as I said, these organizations were shaping the laws that built veterans' benefits at this moment in time. Black veterans were very cognizant of the fact that if they were represented in these organizations, they were going to help shape these laws. The rejection of their calls for membership means they were being shut out of the political process in a very real and conscious way. Indeed, the veterans' health system that was shaped, in part, by veterans' service organizations likewise adopted the "states' rights" credo; veterans' hospitals adopted so-called local practices when it came to setting rules about whether or not care was segregated.[58]

The second example of how southerners shaped this system has to do with the activism of black veterans and black leaders, who used it as a battleground for civil rights. We see that in the case of Tuskegee Veterans' Hospital, which is right here in Alabama. When Tuskegee was being built in the early 1920s, there were really strong efforts by the white community to ensure, as Jennifer Keene and others have written, that the institution would be overseen entirely by white trustees.[59] But black veterans, black doctors, black professionals fought to ensure that that hospital would not operate unless it was managed—top to bottom—by African Americans.

The Tuskegee case gets at the more general point that, once a federal system was built, black activists and black leaders used it to leverage—to chip away at Jim Crow, to chip away at segregation. And they worked, in many cases, with white federal bureaucrats. Black leaders directed the efforts, and white bureaucrats quietly supported them. On the ground level—in military hospitals, in public health service hospitals, and in veterans' hospitals eventually—black veterans and their advocates brought attention to the conditions that they were experiencing by writing to this new federal office, "the VA" or the "Veterans Bureau." They were writing especially, of course, to black newspapers, and they were making the unequal conditions known. And it was their arguments that laid the groundwork for the relatively early desegregation of the veterans' health system.[60] They were in a unique position to be able to say, "This doesn't make sense. You're calling on us to serve our country in the name of freedom and democracy and then also being extremely undemocratic in the ways that you're supporting us thereafter."

So those are my three proposals regarding how the story of veterans' health care relates to the history of the South. It represents a heightened federal presence—a federalization of veterans' benefits—and an important increase in the availability of medical care. And it highlights southerners' ability to shape power dynamics within a new federal bureaucracy.

AUDIENCE: I'm a veteran, to kind of explain my interest in this. How was the term *veteran* defined back then? Did you just have to be army, or did you actually have to serve overseas? How was that defined? Also, the Great War created a huge new population of vets, right? How did those vets feel—does any of your research say what those veterans said about the care they were getting? I ask that question because in my experience veterans are all really unhappy with the care that they get, and today, I think veterans are actually treated pretty well considering how they were treated back then. So how did veterans perceive the care they were getting? Were there a lot of complaints? Were they happy with it? Was this a brand-new day and the government cares about us all of a sudden?

ADLER: My book would've been a lot shorter if veterans were all happy with the care they were getting. So the quick answer is no, at least some were not happy. But I'll take your first question first—regarding the definition of veteran. In terms of access to veterans' benefits, everything was contingent on your discharge type. Ostensibly, you could not access veterans' hospitals if you had a dishonorable discharge. There were so many other debates about other conditions that might increase or decrease access to benefits: for example, the percentage of disability that you incurred in the service, the time that had elapsed between your diagnosis and your discharge, your income level and ability to pay for care elsewhere. But many limiting conditions were gradually, over time, chipped away. The hospitals became, in a variety of ways, more and more accessible. Plus, accessibility was often contingent on the whims of administrators at specific facilities. Some hospital directors, for example, were very lax about requiring proof that prospective patients could not afford care elsewhere. But that dishonorable discharge qualifier was never shaken. So that's an important consideration.

Another important point is that the veterans' health system, and the Veterans' Bureau, initially were set up to serve, really, WWI veterans. An audience member brought up in the earlier panel discussion the topic of Spanish-American War veterans, which begs questions about previous generations and who the system was intended to serve. What you see, mainly among Spanish-American War veterans, is this roar of a desire to be recognized and to be served by entities that seemed to be geared toward young veterans who, from the perspective of aging former service members, were getting everything handed to them. Spanish-American War veterans were wondering why they, too, were not getting these benefits. In fact, Spanish-American War veterans went to Congress and claimed that they tried to go to veterans' hospitals and were rejected because they were not WWI veterans. And legislators responded by saying, "Well, that's not the intention of the law. These are supposed to be open to everyone." But the Spanish-American War veterans ensured that there was a law passed that specifically said that veterans of the Boxer Rebellion, veterans of the Spanish-American War—and all these different categories—would have access to all the supports that had originally been designed for WWI veterans. So, we have definitions of veteran status based on a number of characteristics, including type of discharge and time period of service. And in terms of the perception of care that veterans had . . .

AUDIENCE: Yes, I am thinking of the Bonus March later, in the context of the Great Depression.

ADLER: Well, the Bonus March was a political rally at the height of the Great Depression in 1932, where veterans called on their government to immediately give them the cash bonus that was set to be paid in 1945. In the textbooks, this march is seen as a moment when veterans were shockingly and unfathomably shooed away from the Capitol in a violent way. But if you look at the Bonus March as the middle or end of the story of the WWI fight for benefits, rather than a suspended moment of the Great Depression, it looks different. Because by the 1930s, you had an expansive system of veterans' healthcare—and 80 percent of the people who were getting care had non-service-connected conditions. And there was a lot of talk in letters, in the federal bureaucracy, in the public press, and especially among doctors about the fact that this was actually just a welfare system and that these veterans did not deserve what was being given to them. Government officials and the general public were saying, "Here we are servicing these people who don't have service-connected disabilities and why are we doing this?" If you think about that conversation in relation to the violent government response to the Bonus March, it actually makes sense; there was a fair amount of opposition to this constant cry among veterans for more. People were very much, by the 1930s, tired of it. Especially when there was great economic suffering among the general population.

But in terms of the perceptions of care, it is a complicated question. I would say that some of the same issues, many of the same issues that we hear about today, are evident in the correspondence of veterans from the early 1920s and 1930s, which is to say that they were complaining not just about quality of care but also making very strong arguments about the fact that they should be classified as having service-connected disabilities and that they were very dissatisfied that the government wasn't recognizing that. Having a service-connected disability, after all, not only got you access to a hospital—by the 1930s, you could have access to a veterans' hospital even if you didn't have a service-connected disability—but it also got you a disability compensation check. And so you see this kind of constant adjustment of policy based on how many people were getting or not getting service-connected status. And you see a kind of push and pull between veterans and the bureaucrats who were supposed to be serving them. Really, on a more general level, the Veterans' Bureau representatives were trying to show that they were proactively serving veterans. And then, in the background, legislators were voicing skepticism about the system and saying, "Who are we serving? Are these people worthy?" But there were plenty of very vocal complaints from veterans and, in return, skepticism about whether those complaints were valid.

AUDIENCE: I'd like to address the issue of the flu pandemic to Dr. Bristow. One of the obvious conclusions from her remarks is that we had some 650,000 citizens die of the flu pandemic. This contrasts with 160,000 military deaths, and God knows how many of those military deaths were from the flu. Maybe half of them. A third to a half. And so I'd like to get your reaction to this. The home front barely had time to recover from its home losses, and thus, we neglected the loss of our military men because the suffering at home was as much as five times greater than the military losses. Maybe even ten times greater than those who died in actual combat. Could you comment on whether or not the degree of empathy and understanding of military losses were overshadowed by the flu pandemic crisis?

BRISTOW: I think the opposite was true. When we look at how the memory of the pandemic works you find this very strange phenomenon. And that's why I wanted to end with the idea that the pandemic and the war were conflated. Many people forgot all about the pandemic almost immediately. It left the public sphere. There are only a couple of novels written about it. There's no public attention to the anniversaries. It just disappears, while you had millions of Americans who had lost loved ones or were themselves still suffering the aftereffects of their own illness. And yet the pandemic just disappeared from the public conversation and popular culture.

At the same moment, though, you actually do have memorializing efforts for the war, so at least in a public sense there was far more attention to the war and its consequences than there were to the private consequences of this pandemic. It was always overshadowed by the war. Even at the height of the pandemic, stories about the flu could appear on page 12, page 16 of local newspapers while the war gained banner headlines above the fold on page 1. Only rarely would you find a headline about the flu at the top of the page, even in the smallest local papers. So my sense isn't that the war dead lost their place to the pandemic deaths because the pandemic deaths go almost unremarked. As one further example of the silencing of the pandemic in American public life, Woodrow Wilson never commented on the Spanish flu pandemic. Throughout his time as president of the United States he never commented publicly on it, even in the midst of this terrible scourge. So you raise a really interesting question, one I'm going to have to keep thinking through because certainly it's possible I've missed something. But my immediate response is a bit of the opposite, that the war really gained the attention of the public in a way that the pandemic never did, at least in the public sphere.

AUDIENCE: I would like to add something else to my remarks. In Muscle Shoals, Alabama, we built a large military medical complex. It had as many as one hundred thousand workers that came in, craftsmen coming in waves to build that complex. The records, while not complete, indicate that as many as two thousand people died in the whole community in 1918 related to the flu and a few through industrial accidents. And the number who died included groups that you might not expect. For instance, anecdotal records that had been kept indicated that there were a sizeable number of Cubans who died in the pandemic, and there's a place called Cuban Yards where Cubans were supposedly buried in mass graves. There's also Mexicans who were recruited as part of the workforce that came out of the borderlands, stopping Pancho Villa in 1916. And apparently, those friendlies the army recruited in to help build this complex. So we had really quite a mix. Even though the housing was white housing and colored housing, it's believed that colored included a fair amount of Cubans and Mexicans.

BRISTOW: I really appreciate that information, and I'll add here that there's a scholar, James Higgins, currently at the University of Houston–Victoria, who has done extensive research on the pandemic in Pennsylvania and has been instrumental in the discovery and discussion of mass graves of immigrant populations. He has also been doing research about the thousands of unnamed people of color, especially people from Mexico and Mexican Americans, who died of influenza in the American Southwest. It's a huge part of the story that is desperately under-researched.

AUDIENCE: I know that while we were fighting the Germans in Europe there was also a mass amount of anti-German sentiment in America. For instance, in Dothan, Alabama, there was a company that employed German immigrants that had to change their name because of their affiliation with their home empire. Would any of you elaborate on the treatment of the German American population? And a follow-up question would be two of my ancestors fought in WWI. One fought on the American side, the other fought in the German army—and when one of them returned home, there was some cruel treatment of him because of whom he had fought for.

BRISTOW: I have only a piece of an answer. Americans traditionally have tended to find blame elsewhere for pandemics, so the blaming of the Germans would have been in keeping with a tradition in a sense. But the reality is that—though I can't speak to the South distinctly—nationwide, this does not seem to have been the case. Certainly, as I noted, a handful of Americans saw in the pandemic the workings of a German plot. But overall, there was not a targeting of the German American population or of German immigrants during the pandemic. The expert on this is Alan Kraut, and he found little actual actions against immigrant communities in major urban centers in the United States. This came as actually quite a surprise to many of us that studied the pandemic. That's not to suggest by any means any dismissal of your point, which is this terrible treatment of German and German Americans during the war. It's one of the ugly pieces of that war that we cannot ignore, including lynchings and beatings around the country. But I can't speak to the difference between North and South.

OLLIFF: I can't speak to the difference between North and South either, but I can give you some instances of things that happened in Alabama, for example, pinging off what you indicated happened or you think happened. We know, for example, that in Mobile the German Club of immigrants found an anonymous letter on its front porch saying, "If you don't quit holding your meetings in German then the next anonymous thing you find will be dynamite." And they quit holding their meetings in German. They quit speaking German because that note was deemed, as we would say today, a credible threat. There were lots of instances like that throughout the United States.

Remember this is the time when Progressivism was in high gear. "Progressivism with a capital P isn't necessarily what we think of as lower-case p progressivism today. Currently, progressivism refers to the left wing of contemporary political liberalism, but Progressivism was a pretty specific set of ideas, some of which we would consider today to be backward and xenophobic, that arose in the wake of large-scale immigration. Immigration cranked up in the 1880s and spiked in 1905. So you have three years of anti-German wartime atrocity propaganda combined with even more years of anti-immigrant economic propaganda—what we might hear on *South Park* as "they got our jobs!" So xenophobia began to crank up with immigration. The Second Klan formed in 1915, and even though it was initially aimed at white supremacist suppression of African Americans, it very quickly morphed into "100 percent Americanism," which is an ugly side of the Americanist project. Jane Addams was an Americanist, but she believed we could *educate* people to be better Americans. We could *educate* immigrants to be Americans. One hundred percent Americanism believed we could *make* immigrants become Americans or *make* them hide whatever they were doing that wasn't "American," that we could *force* Americanism. This was the hard edge of the Americanist movement. There was a large emigration of foreign nationals from the United States because of the war. People went back to fight for their national armies. I can't tell you numbers, but I suspect that lots of these folks left Alabama and the South in general, where they had not lived in large numbers except in the South's few-and-far-between industrialized cities. But there has always been in Alabama a *slight* closed-mindedness to outside ideas and outside people, and even though people tell you that violence won't solve your problems, many people believe violence and the threat of violence solved this Americanization problem. With the threat of violence, the dominant members of society can enforce pretty much whatever they want to enforce. And what they wanted to enforce was 100 percent Americanism.

AUDIENCE: My first question is why the memory of the pandemic faded so quickly. And second, why is it that every TV show or movie now features some sort of virus that leads to the destruction of humanity? Is it related to the post-9/11 world?

BRISTOW: I would add a few things to our thinking about where the memory went. It's not only that it's conflated with the war, although I think that's essential to its disappearance. There are a couple of other pieces that I think are worth mentioning. One is the point I made earlier that the pandemic did not cause dramatic changes in American culture. In other words, most people acted according to their norms during the pandemic. Cultural practices—like white Americans clinging to segregation or women seeing themselves as caregivers and male doctors seeing themselves as people who should be able to cure disease—didn't change despite the pandemic. This was true despite the resistance of some communities, including the African American community, to the ongoing discrimination they faced. So when it came to remembering the pandemic, there was nothing to look to in terms of how the nation changed except for those 675,000 deaths. It didn't leave any social, cultural, economic, or political markers that demanded its remembrance.

And my last point is that the pandemic doesn't fit with the story Americans were telling about themselves in 1918. Americans saw themselves as victors in the war. We were a burgeoning world power. We were a scientific nation that was building new hospitals. Doctors, nurses, public health experts, nobody wanted to confront the reality that this was a tremendous failure in terms of our capacities to deal with pandemic infectious disease. And so the pandemic faded under the war as Americans refused to incorporate the pandemic into their view of themselves.

Now the question about the resurgence of interest is a really wonderful question. I don't have an easy answer to it. I would point out that the resurgence in interest in the 1918 pandemic among scholars preceded the resurgence in popular culture. The new generation of what one colleague calls "flu-storians" emerged worldwide, a reality made clear in 1998 with the eightieth anniversary conference held at the University of Cape Town in South Africa. There were people from all over the world there, including many who were doing the very first research in their countries such as India and Mauritius. I think the scholarly interest has grown out of changes in the field of the history of medicine, as scholars moved beyond the study of great doctors and medical organizations and institutions and began reflecting on other developments in the discipline of history, for instance social history. Now in terms of popular culture, it is as if pandemics have gotten kind of sexy, and I think you may well be right that it has to do with post-9/11. That's a really interesting idea, and one I want to think much more about, and of course, others are welcome to comment.

AUDIENCE: So, do scholars bear responsibility for the popularity of *The Walking Dead?*

BRISTOW: No. Well, it would be pretty amazing if we are responsible. Pop culture doesn't generally grab hold of our books and run with them.

AUDIENCE: So I have a comment and a question about how things were lining up in terms of thinking about segregated hospitals both during and after the war. And I think that it's been interesting, through my research, to see things like segregation in military hospitals especially and that doctors didn't say anything about disease when grouping patients. The second thing I would say is that I've done some work on Tuskegee when they created a segregated hospital there. There was this group within the African American community that debated whether and how it benefited black doctors and black nurses to have government positions. And then the third thing, and this is actually more a question to put out there for discussion, is that I've also read accounts where families argue that when you're sick and you're very vulnerable you want to be treated by somebody who's interested in treating you and who's kind and compassionate to you and that it was traumatic for many black patients to be treated in a hospital by racist doctors. So families provided care to their loved ones.

ADLER: I'll start with the first question about this idea of segregation and how it worked. As some here know, the military during WWI did begin with the policy that Jennifer Keene mentioned: organizing patients in hospitals based on their conditions, disabilities, or illnesses. Scientific and medical considerations, in other words, took precedent over ideals about the virtues of segregation. But what ended up happening was there were complaints from white soldiers who were saying they didn't want to be housed in the same wards, definitely not next to beds, with black soldiers. And so what you see is a gradual accommodation of this perspective and a prioritization of the social concerns of white soldiers over the actual health of black soldiers. And you see this kind of piecemeal adoption of segregation as an unofficial policy. And this varied based on, in my understanding, the individual perspectives of the hospital commander and his feelings about how the issue should be addressed. And so you see this gradual accommodation of a system of segregation. And you see a heightening of fighting back on the part of black soldiers who were enduring this.[61]

Regarding the point, and I want to let Nancy speak to all of these things, too, but just quickly regarding your point about segregated hospitals in general and Tuskegee's role in this conversation, you're right to say that in the early 1920s, you see great debate among black leaders as to whether segregation was a step forward or back. And one thing that everybody could agree upon was that having a white hospital commander over an all-black staff was definitely not a good idea. So whether you thought segregation could work or not, that was definitely not going to happen. But in the early 1930s, long after activists had won the fight to ensure that Tuskegee would be overseen by an all-black staff, some black doctors were actually calling for the creation of a second all-black veterans' hospital. You see the debate unfold in the *Journal of the National Medical Association*, the publication of the national organization of African American doctors.[62] But within about ten years, in the pages of that same journal, you see black doctors saying, "No—no more of this. Integration and equal care is the only way forward."[63] This, I think, corresponds with a larger turn away from the idea of segregation and an adopting wholesale of the original NAACP argument that you cannot segregate and have equality. By the 1940s, black doctors, too, were on board with this idea, and they said, "no more all black veterans' hospitals. The only fight is for the full integration of the veterans' health system." And they were meeting and reporting on their meetings with Veterans Administration officials in the *Journal of the National Medical Association*, saying, "We've met with different people who are heading this veterans' health system, and we're fighting only for integration at this point." I think the argument for having a segregated hospital is very powerful; you're talking about bodies and you're talking about states like Alabama that have laws on the books saying that white nurses could refuse to treat black patients if they wanted to. And so they had to do something in the face of that. But the question was what to do. That was an open debate, I think, in these years.

BRISTOW: I just want to add that your point about who is caring for whom is crucial. In the midst of the pandemic the people who are really doing the caregiving were nurses. And nurses were almost exclusively female. It was, in fact, the flu pandemic that made it possible for African American nurses to serve in the American armed forces. Before that they had been excluded despite their best efforts to be included. In one of the typical twists of segregation, African American women were permitted to care for white men, reproducing the history of African American women serving white people and serving in white homes.

But I think it is really important to notice the way in which any opportunity felt like an opportunity in 1918; so despite the kinds of segregation that people faced, to have the opportunity, for instance, to serve in the US military was a big deal. I would also mention that in the midst of the pandemic there was a great deal of resistance from the African American community fighting against these problems of segregation and also attempting to shape the way the pandemic was being understood and narrated. So at least in the civilian realm, there was not an acceptance of the segregation but a fighting back pretty routinely. As African American women accepted positions in the segregated military, we should understand that they were glad to have this opportunity, but this did not imply any agreement with segregation.

AUDIENCE: I just wanted to ask a question about the war overshadowing sickness, the pandemic. Do you believe that people in the military who died on American soil [from the flu] helped others to grieve and understand and then care about their deaths?

BRISTOW: One thing I would point out is that of the soldiers who died, more than half of them died in camps stateside. They were actually in the United States. Somewhere over thirty thousand of the soldiers who died of influenza or of pneumonia actually weren't in Europe; they were here in the United States. So, again, I don't think the war deaths were forgotten. I think the pandemic deaths were forgotten. Why does the war itself eventually become a forgotten war? It wasn't forgotten originally. Think of all the literature produced about the war or public responses like the creation of the VA. The most obvious reason for the loss of the memory of the Great War is the coming of a second great war that's even more horrific.

NOTES

1. Page Smith, *America Enters the World* (New York: McGraw-Hill, 1985), 414–15; Arthur S. Link, *Woodrow Wilson and the Progressive Era, 1910–1917* (New York: Harper and Row, 1954), 63–66.

2. Obviously, the War Department named the camp for General George McClellan, commander of the Union Army of the Potomac during the US Civil War.

3. Hermann Hagedorn, *Leonard Wood: A Biography*, 2 vol. (New York: Kraus Reprint, 1969), 2:223.

4. "Dent, Stanley Hubert, Jr., (1869–1938)," Biographical Dictionary of the United States Congress, 1774–Present," bioguide.congress.gov; Robert D. Ward, "Stanley Hubert Dent and American Military Policy, 1916–1920," *Alabama Historical Quarterly* 33 (Fall/Winter 1971): 177, 180.

5. E. L. May, *Souvenir History of Camp Sheridan, Montgomery, Ala.* (Montgomery, AL: n.p., 1918), 73–77.

6. May, *Souvenir History of Camp Sheridan*, 73–78, 117–18; Wesley P. Newton, "'Tenting Tonight on the Old Camp Grounds': Alabama's Military Bases in World War I," in *The Great War in the Heart of Dixie: Alabama during World War I*, ed. Martin T. Olliff (Tuscaloosa: University of Alabama Press, 2008), 42–45.

7. May, *Souvenir History of Camp Sheridan*, 122; Samuel H. Williamson, "Seven Ways to Compute the Relative Value of a U.S. Dollar Amount, 1774 to present," Measuring Worth, 2018, www.measuringworth.com.

8. Newton, "'Tenting Tonight,'" 56–59.

9. Newton, "'Tenting Tonight,'" 50–55, 59–62; Grace Hooten Gates, *The Model City of the New South—Anniston, Alabama, 1872–1900* (Huntsville, AL: Strode Publishers, 1978), 140–43; Joseph H. Ewing, *29th Infantry Division: A Short History of a Fighting Division* (Nashville: Turner Publishing, 1992), 11–12; Richard J. Connors, *New Jersey and the Great War: 1914–1919* (Pittsburgh: Dorrance Publishing, 2017), 103–4.

10. Mr. Mize and Mr. Sheridan were in the audience.

11. Victoria E. Ott, "From the Cotton Fields to the Great Waterway: African Americans and the Muscle Shoals Project during World War I," in Olliff, *Great War*, 101–20.

12. Williamson, "Seven Ways to Compute."

13. Michael Thomason, "Mobile in World War I," in Olliff, *Great War*, 128–29; "Mobile's Piers in the Bridge to France," *Electric Railway Journal*, June 22, 1918, 1185–86; Christopher MacGregor Scribner, "Progress and Tradition in Mobile, 1900–1920," in *Mobile: The New History of Alabama's First City*, ed. Michael Thomason (Tuscaloosa: University of Alabama Press, 2001), 155–80.

14. Matthew L. Downs, "'The Battle for Commerce Is Begun': World War I and the Impetus for Industrial Development in Mobile, Alabama," in *The American South and the Great War: 1914–1924*, ed. Matthew L. Downs and M. Ryan Floyd (Baton Rouge: Louisiana State University Press, 2018).

15. John S. Sledge, *The Mobile River* (Columbia: University of South Carolina Press, 2015), 185–87; Thomason, "Mobile in World War I," 128–30.

16. "What Shipping Means to Mobile," *American Shipping*, February 10, 1921, 48; Williamson, "Seven Ways to Compute."

17. Private Josh Lee, "The Flu," quoted in Peter C. Weaver and Leo van Bergen, "Death from 1918 Pandemic Influenza during the First World War: A Perspective from Personal and Anecdotal Evidence," *Influenza and Other Respiratory Viruses* 8:5 (September 2014): 538–46, available online at www.ncbi.nlm.nih.gov.

18. Niall P. A. S. Johnson and Juergen Mueller, "Updating the Accounts: Global Mortality of the 1918–1920 'Spanish' Influenza Pandemic," *Bulletin of the History of Medicine* 76 (Spring 2002): 107, 114–15; Jeffery K. Taubenberger and David M. Morens, "1918 Influenza: The Mother of All Pandemics," *Emerging Infectious Diseases* 12 (January 2006): 15; Jeffery K. Taubenberger and David M. Morens, "Influenza: The Once and Future Pandemic," *Public Health Reports* 125 (2010, Supplement 3): 19–20.

19. Nancy K. Bristow, *American Pandemic: The Lost Worlds of the 1918 Influenza Pandemic* (New York: Oxford University Press, 2012), chap. 1.

20. "Birmingham, Alabama," *Influenza Encyclopedia—The American Influenza Epidemic of 1918–1919: A Digital Encyclopedia*, www.influenzaarchive.org.

21. Taubenberger and Morens, "Influenza," 20–21.

22. Bristow, *American Pandemic*, chaps. 2, 3, and 4.

23. Taubenberger and Morens, "Influenza," 20; Taubenberger and Morens, "1918 Influenza," 15.

24. "The Influenza Epidemic of 1918 in the South—The Great Flu Disaster of 1918," available on the ExploreSouthernHistory.com website, www.exploresouthernhistory.com.

25. "Nashville, Tennessee," "Atlanta, Georgia," *Influenza Encyclopedia*, www.influenza archive.org.

26. "New Orleans, Louisiana," *Influenza Encyclopedia*, www.influenzaarchive.org.

27. "The Influenza Epidemic of 1918 in the South—The Great Flu Disaster of 1918," www .exploresouthernhistory.com.

28. "Therapeutics—Epidemic Influenza," *Journal of the American Medical Association* (hereafter *JAMA*) 71 (October 5, 1918): 1136; George A. Soper, "Military Medicine and Surgery—The Pandemic in the Army Camps," *JAMA* 71 (December 7, 1918): 1901; E. R. LeCount, "The Pathologic Anatomy of Influenza Bronchopneumonia," *JAMA* 72 (March 1, 1919): 650; M. W. Lyon Jr., "Gross Pathology of Epidemic Influenza at Walter Reed General Hospital," *JAMA* 72 (March 29, 1919): 925.

29. Clifford Adams, quoted in John Barry, *The Great Influenza: The Epic Story of the Deadliest Plague in History* (New York: Viking, 2004), 232.

30. For a full account of the circumstances of patients, their families, and their communities, see Bristow, *American Pandemic*, chap. 2.

31. Samuel Kelton Roberts Jr., *Infectious Fear: Politics, Disease, and the Health Effects of Segregation* (Chapel Hill: University of North Carolina Press, 2009), 4, 34–35, 68–70.

32. "Birmingham, Alabama," *Influenza Encyclopedia*.

33. Marian Moser Jones, "The American Red Cross and Local Response to the 1918 Influenza Pandemic: A Four-City Case Study," *Public Health Reports* 125 (2010, Supplement 3): 101; Vanessa Northington Gamble, "'There Wasn't A Lot of Comforts in Those Days': African Americans, Public Health, and the 1918 Influenza Epidemic," *Public Health Reports* 125 (2010, Supplement 3): 119.

34. Gamble, "'There Wasn't A Lot of Comforts,'" 119.

35. See for instance case #13906, Reel #197, Family Welfare, Minneapolis Family and Children's Service Case Records, 1895–1945, Social Welfare History Archives, University of Minnesota Libraries; Oscar Jewell Harvey, *The Spanish Influenza Pandemic of 1918: An Account of Its Ravages in Luzerne County, Pennsylvania, and the Efforts Made to Combat and Subdue It* (Wilkes-Barre, PA: n.p, 1920), 45–49.

36. Starr Cadwallader, Division Director, Civilian Relief, Lake Division, to James L. Fieser, Association Director General National Headquarters, August 12, 1919, "Report of the Department of Civilian Relief," "Lake Division—Civilian Relief Reports—July–December 1918," File 149.18, Box 216, Entry 27130D, Record Group 200, National Archives II at College Park, MD.

37. "Report of Mrs. Ella May Huber and Mrs. C. A. Dolan, Who Went to Pineville, Bell Co., Ky. to Nurse Influenza," "Epidemics, Influenza—Reports and Statistics—Lake Division," File 803.08, Box 688, Record Group 200, National Archives II at College Park, MD.

38. John M. Barry, "The Site of Origin of the 1918 Influenza Pandemic and Its Public Health Implications," *Journal of Translational Medicine* (published online January 20, 2004),

www.ncbi.nlm.nih.gov; Dan Vergano, "Influenza Pandemic That Killed 50 Million Originated in China, Historians Say," *National Geographic* (January 24, 2014), news.national geographic.com.

39. Alfred W. Crosby, *America's Forgotten Pandemic: The Influenza of 1918* (New York: Cambridge University Press, 1989), 50–51, 71, 96–97.

40. See for instance questionnaire of H. Louis Brooks, Twelfth Division, Forty-Second Infantry, American Experiences Questionnaire Collection, World War One Research Project, US Army Military History Institute, Carlisle Barracks; Interview with Josie Mabel Brown, "A Winding Sheet and a Wooden Box," *Navy Medicine* 77 (May–June 1986): 18–19, www.history.navy.mil. For a full account of the pandemic in the American military, see Carol R. Byerly, *Fever of War: The Influenza Epidemic in the U. S. Army during World War I* (New York: New York University Press, 2005).

41. Connecticut Department of Health and the Council of National Defense, "Help Fight the Grippe," Broadside 1918, H44, Special Collections Department, University of Virginia Library.

42. For a fuller treatment of this strategy see Bristow, *American Pandemic*, 102–3.

43. Letter of B. R. Hart, Chief, Eastern District to Chief, Bureau of Chemistry, October 28, 1918, and Letter, Assistant Surgeon General to B. R. Hart, November 15, 1918, both in File 1622, Box 144, Record Group 90, National Archives II at College Park, MD. See also Bristow, *American Pandemic*, 76–77.

44. "Wallace Youth Dies Suddenly—Harry R. Kinkead Victim of Pneumonia Which Follows Influenza Attack," *Wallace Press Times, October 29, 1918, 1;* "Will the 'Flu' Return?" *Literary Digest*, 63 (October 11, 1919), 26; "Uncle Sam's Advice on Flu," *Shenandoah Valley* (New Market, VA), October 17, 1918, 1; Wesley T. Lee, *The Battle of Pougues-Lels-Eaux: A History of U.S. Army Base Hospital No. 44* (New York: Globe Press, 1923), 41; News Release #2659 "Released for Morning Papers of Sunday September 29th," contained in bound volume: News Releases Nos. 1861–2821, 1918, vol. III, file 020.1801. News Releases, box 4, entry 27130D, Record Group 200, National Archives II; "How to Fight Spanish Influenza," *Literary Digest* 59 (October 12, 1918), 13–14; Letter from Hugh to "Folks," no date, folder 9—Correspondence September–October 1918, box 1, Hugh Arthur Barnhart Manuscript Collection, Manuscript Section, Indiana State Library; George M. Price, "Influenza—Destroyer and Teacher," *Survey* 41 (December 21, 1919): 367; Editorial, "Influenza Masks," *Daily Californian* (University of California, Berkeley), October 22, 1918, 2, all included in Bristow, *American Pandemic*, 77–78.

45. Portia B. Kernodle, *The Red Cross Nurse in Action* (New York: Harper Bros., 1949), 147.

46. "Our Workers Who Lost Their Lives Fighting the Influenza Epidemic—A Civilian Role of Honor," *Staff News* 6 (December 1, 1918): 1.

47. *Corks and Curls* (UVA Yearbook), 32 (1919).

48. "Epidemic Claims 926 Here," *Camp Sherman News*, October 15, 1918, 1.

49. See Bristow, *American Pandemic*, 178–90.

50. *Annual Report of the Administrator of Veterans' Affairs for the Fiscal Year Ended June 30, 1941* (Washington, DC: GPO, 1941), 44–47, 107–9.

51. Jessica L. Adler, *Burdens of War: Creating the United States Veterans Health System* (Baltimore: Johns Hopkins University Press, 2017).

52. The Spanish-American War was an important post–Civil War moment when national unity was wrought by war and when the federal government recognized southern veterans. See, for example, Richard E. Wood, "The South and Reunion, 1898," *Historian* 31, no. 3 (1969): 415–30. But World War I, by virtue of the numbers that enlisted and were impacted, and the fact that a new bureaucracy (the VA) was established in its wake, was a crucial moment of genesis.

53. W. E. B. Du Bois, *The Health and Physique of the Negro American: Report of a Social Study Made under the Direction of Atlanta University* (Atlanta: University of Atlanta Press, 1906); W. Montague Cobb, *Medical Care and the Plight of the Negro* (New York: National Association for the Advancement of Colored People, 1947).

54. See, for example, Robert Saunders Jr., "World War I: Catalyst for Social Change in Alabama" in Olliff, *Great War*, 185–200.

55. Charles E. Rosenberg, *The Care of Strangers: The Rise of America's Hospital System* (New York: Basic Books, 1987), 121, 5.

56. *Report on Economic Conditions of the South 1938* (Washington, DC: Government Printing Office, 1938), 30.

57. Adler, *Burdens of War*, 149–52.

58. Adler, *Burdens of War*, 211.

59. On Tuskegee, Jennifer D. Keene, "The Long Journey Home: Federal Veterans' Policy and African-American Veterans of World War I," in *Veterans' Policies, Veterans' Politics: New Perspectives on Veterans in the Modern United States*, ed. Stephen Ortiz (Gainesville: University Press of Florida, 2012). Also, Pete Daniel, "Black Power in the 1920s: The Case of Tuskegee Veterans Hospital," *Journal of Southern History* 36, no. 2 (1970): 368–88. On efforts and debates surrounding the creation of all-black hospitals, see Vanessa Northington Gamble, *Making a Place for Ourselves: The Black Hospital Movement, 1920–1945* (New York: Oxford University Press, 1995), which includes a discussion of Tuskegee, 183–86.

60. On the desegregation of veterans' hospitals, see Karen Kruse Thomas, *Deluxe Jim Crow: Civil Rights and American Health Policy, 1935–1954* (Athens, University of Georgia Press, 2011), 167–68; Gamble, *Making a Place for Ourselves*, 185–86; E. H. Beardsley, "Good-Bye to Jim Crow: The Desegregation of Southern Hospitals, 1945–1970," in *Readings in American Health Care*, ed. William G. Rothstein (Madison: University of Wisconsin Press, 1995), 256–57.

61. Adler, "The Service I Rendered Was Just as True: African American Soldiers and Veterans as Activist Patients," *American Journal of Public Health*, 107, no. 5 (2017): 675–83.

62. In 1932, the president of the National Medical Association, Peter Marshall Murray, wrote in the *Journal of the National Medical Association*: "The fact remains that the majority of Negro veterans must look for hospitalization in institutions in the south. . . . Negro veterans will find themselves in Jim Crow wards attached to southern white veterans' institutions. . . . The record of Hospital No. 91 [Tuskegee Veterans' Hospital] under an all Negro personnel has demonstrated that they will be better cared for and happier in another such unit under

complete Negro personnel. . . . We challenge the National Association for the Advancement of Colored People to join hands with the National Medical Association in this constructive program," Peter Marshall Murray, "The President's Column," *Journal of the National Medical Association* 24, no. 2 (1932): 48–49.

63. By January 1946, the *Journal of the National Medical Association* reported that the National Medical Association, NAACP, and other black advocacy groups had met with Veterans' Bureau officials about the necessity of integration and their vehement disapproval of conditions as they stood. A. C. Terrence, "The Problem of Veterans' Facilities," *Journal of the National Medical Association* 38, no. 1 (1946): 37. Also, Roscoe C. Giles, "Post-War Adjustments in Medicine," *Journal of the National Medical Association* 38, no. 4 (1946): 126–27.

3

Fighting the Great War Over There

RUTH SMITH TRUSS, KARA DIXON VUIC, AND CHAD L. WILLIAMS

Large numbers of Americans went overseas to fight in the First World War—and their experiences both provoked and reflected larger developments in American so-cial, cultural, and political life. Much of the discussion with Ruth Smith Truss, Kara Dixon Vuic, and Chad Williams focused on the lives of women and people of color in the war zone, following the scholarly literature in suggesting that the war both advanced and undermined broader campaigns for civil, social, and po-litical rights. Yet it was the gender and race of many of these Americans, Vuic and Williams suggested, more than their southern roots, that dictated the ways they experienced the war—and the ways American officials imagined, manipulated, and sometimes denigrated their service. For Truss, on the other hand, the south-ern character of the Alabamians in the 167th Infantry Regiment influenced much, though not all, of their wartime experiences. Audience members asked for further discussion of African American women and for the panelists to connect their re-marks to European colonial racism, the Harlem Renaissance, the contradictions of black service in a war for "democracy," the explosive sexual/racial politics of the period, and the broader environment of white supremacy.

CHAD WILLIAMS: I'm going to focus on what it meant for black ser-vicemen, and specifically black servicemen from the South, to be over there during the First World War.[1] In what ways was their experience in France different? In which ways was it new? In which ways was it broadening? But at the same time, in what ways was it not new? In what ways did the South travel with these men to France, over there? I'd like for us to really grapple with that tension in particular and to also think about what it potentially meant for the experiences of black servicemen in the postwar period, which has been touched upon a little bit in the last session, and also what it means in terms of the history and memory of the war, anticipating the panel after ours.

Some facts and figures just to frame my comments and get us all on the same page in terms of what we're talking about and who we're talking about. Roughly 380,000 African Americans served in World War I, and roughly 200,000 served overseas in France. As was said before, the majority of black servicemen served as laborers, both in the United States as well as overseas. And just to briefly take a step back, I think it's important to consider the experiences of those soldiers who did not travel to France, the roughly 180,000 black soldiers who stayed at home for various reasons, and what their experiences were and what it meant in terms of their identity as soldiers to not have the opportunity to serve overseas in France. But for those men who did serve overseas in France: although the vast majority did serve in labor units, there were two black combat divisions, the Ninety-Second Division, which was composed of men drafted by the Selective Service system, and the Ninety-Third Division, which was composed predominately of black National Guardsmen. The Ninety-Third Division had a unique experience because they did not serve in the American Expeditionary Forces [AEF] but instead served with the French military.

On the whole, black servicemen who did travel overseas had experiences in France that were truly life altering. It was a disjunctive experience, and it's important to remember that the vast majority of these men serving in France were indeed from the South. The overwhelming majority of black men who were drafted into the military came from the South, and the overwhelming majority of black labor troops came from the South as well.

When thinking about the lives of these individuals, I want us to remember the circumscribed nature of their lives and experiences prior to entering the military. These were individuals who by and large had not traveled far beyond their homes, their towns, their farms. Their lives and experiences were defined in a very localized way. And that was also reflective of their circumscribed citizenship status as well. African Americans during the First World War were effectively citizens in name only. This was the height of Jim Crow America, or the "nadir" of race relations as Rayford Logan, a veteran of the war himself, termed it.[2] So the war represented a remarkable opportunity for African Americans and black servicemen from the South specifically. This was an opportunity for black men and black women from the South—we haven't really touched upon the experiences of women and gender in the war, hopefully we can do that—but this represented an opportunity for black southerners to stake claim to their citizenship in a very concrete way, by using the civic obligation of military service as a way to reinforce what they already knew, that they were indeed American citizens and to make that an effective reality as well.

Traveling overseas exposed black servicemen from the South to a different world. It reinforced the fact that the world was bigger than the South. And this was critical in terms of expanding their consciousness on a whole host of different levels. So there are a few things that I'd just like to quickly discuss and point out in terms of the ways in which black servicemen from the South were transformed by their experience over there and the significance of it.

The first was the opportunity to meet other black people. Again, it is important to emphasize that not all black people were the same, that not all black southerners were the same. We tend to use this catchall phrase "black southerners" when in fact we should be thinking about the tremendous diversity that existed among black southerners and among black Americans more broadly at this particular time. In the military, soldiers had the opportunity to meet black men from other regions of the South, to interact with black men from different socioeconomic positions, black men from different ideological and political/religious beliefs and perspectives, and then the opportunity to meet black men from the North, from other parts of the country. So this was a key aspect of the broadened racial consciousness that black soldiers experienced throughout their process of being in the military and certainly as they traveled overseas in France and experienced life over there.

Connected to that, a second issue is the interactions that black southerners had with African soldiers. This was a world war as W. E. B. Du Bois argued as early as 1914. The war was about empire. The roots of the war lay in Africa and the imperial competition among Germany, France, England, and Belgium for its economic and human resources, as Du Bois argued in a seminal 1915 essay in the *Atlantic Monthly*.[3] The various European belligerents made use of African troops in different theaters and in different ways. The French specifically made extensive use of their colonial troops from West and North Africa, and African American troops had the opportunity to interact with these individuals, interact with these colonial troops in the context of labor service but also in the context of combat. This was remarkable. Imagine, for example, a black sharecropper from Alabama finding himself on a transport ship and then in France and experiencing the sight of colonial troops from Africa laboring or fighting alongside him. This was a profound moment in terms of a broadening diasporic—dare I say even Pan-African—consciousness. But it also exposed the particular Americanness of African American troops, exposed how they saw the distinctions between themselves and their African counterparts in ways that oftentimes reinforced their Americanness. So there was this kind of diasporic component to their overseas experiences as well.[4]

Connected to that were their experiences with white French men and women. The story is often told that the French public embraced African Americans with open arms, that this was an example of the colorblind nature of France and French racial egalitarianism in practice. And there are certainly some elements of truth to that. The French were eager for any type of assistance that they could have at this stage in the war. They oftentimes did in fact welcome African American soldiers into their homes. There was a real social as well as military bond on the battlefield, particularly between French officers and black troops. However, I certainly don't want to reinforce the idea that France was devoid of racism.[5]

Related to the experiences of black soldiers interacting with the French was their exposure to new ideas. For the graduate students here, a great potential dissertation would consider the intellectual history of the experience of southern soldiers in the war and what it meant to be exposed to new and potentially radical ideas, what it meant to be engaged in a war for democracy, what it meant to be exposed to a system of race relations that was fundamentally different from what they experienced in the South. What did it mean to internalize the idea that the French were different from Americans and that race had a different set of possibilities when outside of the United States? How did this exposure to a different set of ideas for black servicemen—regardless of their service roles—become internalized in them, and how did it shape their consciousness in terms of their relationship to the United States?

Those are just some of the ways that I think the experience of being over there was transformative, was new, was broadening for black southern troops. But then there's this other side of the history, the way in which their experience over there was very similar to their experiences here, how American white supremacy and even more poignantly how southern white supremacy was transported from the United States to France. White supremacy was not tangential to the history of the American experience in the war. It was not something that was just transported by a few bad apples in the American Expeditionary Forces but something that was central to how the American army was organized and how the United States went about waging war. Southern white supremacy was central to the American war effort. So in this sense, black southerners never really left the South because the South traveled with them in a whole host of different ways.

I'd like to quickly point out some examples of how white supremacy and the racism of the southern experience transferred to France. First is the experience of black soldiers as laborers, the idea that black men were particularly suited as a result of their so-called natural capabilities for labor service.

As was mentioned earlier, the US Army made the concerted decision very early on that black soldiers were going to be used almost exclusively in a labor capacity, that they were going to be effectively "laborers in uniform" to quote documents of the time. The military—which as was also mentioned was dominated by white southerners—made the point that they were not going to address the "race question." Even though Secretary of War Newton Baker was a northerner from Cleveland, a "good progressive" we might say, he was adamant in not disturbing the customs of the South. He didn't want to anger the southern white hierarchy that controlled the army, so he went along with the traditions and practices of the US military, and that meant using black soldiers largely as laborers. And that affected their experiences in very acute ways, whether it was their susceptibility to influenza or the harsh conditions that they had to endure as stevedores or digging ditches or burying dead bodies. All this ugly, unglamorous work of the war was still obviously vital to the American war effort, but was demeaning nevertheless, and again challenged these individuals in terms of their identities as soldiers. They wanted to be carrying guns instead of shovels.

Next, Jim Crow policies were instituted within the military top to bottom, with Jim Crow justified as a matter of military efficiency. One of the ironies of the war effort, one that affected both the military and social experiences of black soldiers, whether it was being segregated in hospital wards to actually being segregated on the battlefield—was that this was all done in the cause of military efficiency.

Another really important part of the experience of black soldiers overseas in France was sex. The sexualized nature of southern white supremacy was transferred to France as well. James Vardaman, who was brought up earlier—I hate that guy—he warned of "French-woman-ruined negro soldiers" serving overseas and coming back to the South and dreaded what that would mean for race relations during the war and particularly during the postwar period. So the fears that existed, the type of anxieties that existed around the presence of black soldiers in France was highly sexualized in terms of their relationships and access to French women and what that could potentially mean for postwar relations back in the South. The Ninety-Second Division was falsely accused of being guilty of a disproportionate number of rapes while serving overseas in France, so this discourse of black men as habitual rapists carried over into the experiences of black soldiers overseas. The Ninety-Second Division was actually labeled the "raping division." The number of soldiers executed on French soil specifically for charges of rape disproportionately lent toward African American troops. So the experiences of justice were highly sexualized as well.

This leads to my final point, the presence of violence. Black soldiers had violence inflicted upon them physically, in terms of the demeaning treatment that they received particularly as labor troops—there are a whole host of examples that I could point to—but they also experienced psychological and psychic violence. When we think about trauma, oftentimes we think about it in terms of physical wounds, but in the case of black servicemen, white supremacy and American racism acted as a form of violence and trauma that black soldiers suffered from as well.

I think this violence also speaks to the type of violence that was and perhaps continues to be done to the historical memory of black soldiers and their place in the history of the war. For example, Robert Lee Bullard, let me repeat his name: Robert Lee Bullard, from the state of Alabama, major general of the First Infantry Division, one of the highest-ranking officers in the American Expeditionary Forces, commander of the US Army Second Division, underneath which the Ninety-Second Division fell. He wrote in his 1925 memoir that his memories of black troops and the Ninety-Second Division specifically were a nightmare. He said that if you want combat troops and if you want them in a hurry, don't waste your time on black soldiers.[6] This view of black soldiers as being failures, as being ineffective, as not having any significant place in the history of the war—it has affected the historiography of black military service and the larger black experience in the war but also affected the way that we think about the specific experiences of black southerners.

So I would prefer to not focus on the voices and memories of individuals like Robert Lee Bullard but to think about how we can explore the history and memory of the war from the perspective of black southerners themselves. We must find ways to think about how their experiences were transformative or were a continuation of a racial status quo. Such a perspective could and should shape our future studies of the black experience in the war.

KARA DIXON VUIC: World War I had similarly mixed results for American women. The war created many new opportunities for women to serve, at home and in Europe, in the military and as civilians, and it ultimately led to women finally getting the right to vote. But it also reaffirmed many conventional understandings of what women were to be and what they were to do during war. So, like for African Americans, the war was simultaneously transformative and not transformative.

Women went over there in many capacities: as nurses in the Army Nurse Corps, as switchboard operators (or "Hello Girls") in the Army's Signal

Corps, as physicians who funded their own hospitals because the military wouldn't accept women physicians, as volunteers in countless relief organizations.[7] My work focuses on a group of about 3,500 women who went to France with the YMCA and Salvation Army to serve donuts and coffee and make small talk with doughboys. In France (and for some who stayed after the war with the American military in the Rhineland), the women operated huts and canteens that sold tobacco and hot chocolate, served coffee and donuts, organized musical performances and dances, and made small talk with lonely doughboys. Some worked in leave areas, former resorts the Americans operated for soldiers who received a week of leave. Some women even patrolled large cities in an effort to stop men from soliciting prostitutes.[8]

It might seem like an outlandish idea today—sending young women to a war zone to chit chat with soldiers fighting a war—but the Progressive Era civilians who ran the recreation programs and the military leaders who relied on the women all believed that this work was essential to keeping young soldiers and sailors out of trouble. Young women and donuts might not have had the effect that military and civilian leaders hoped for, but they did begin a long history of women going to war to entertain soldiers, to provide for their recreational needs. The women in World War I are essentially the forerunners of women who later went to war with organizations like the USO and Red Cross in World War II, Korea, Vietnam, Iraq, and even today in Afghanistan.

Where did the idea come from? Before World War I, most Americans thought that enlisted soldiers were rough and tumble men who engaged in all sorts of disreputable extracurricular activities, and in many ways, they were right. Sensational stories of army-sponsored prostitution came out of expeditions on the Mexican border, as had appalling rates of venereal disease. But few Americans outside of Progressive organizations really cared. Their sons weren't in the military; they didn't know men who enlisted. That is, until the Selective Service Act of 1917 threatened to conscript a cross section of American boys. Families all over the country all of a sudden worried a great deal about what might happen when their sons were taken from their homes and sent to military camps. They especially worried when those sons were sent to what many considered the land of debauchery, France. And remember that the draft was very unpopular, particularly among southerners, and so the War Department needed to address public fears that military service might corrupt their boys.[9]

In the overly optimistic spirit of the Progressive Era, organizations like the YMCA, Jewish Welfare Board, Knights of Columbus, Salvation Army, and Commission on Training Camp Activities [CTCA] decided that if they could provide soldiers with a wholesome environment, the men would behave themselves, and so they provided a whole range of morale-boosting amusements at training camps and stations across the country.[10] Their efforts were part of a larger, concerted attempt on the part of the government to make military service palatable to the public.

Women were essential to this work, especially in France, for two reasons. The first was to keep the doughboys away from prostitutes and, simultaneously, the thought went, free from venereal disease. Military medical officials convinced Gen. John Pershing, who had condoned prostitution as a necessary evil before the war, that to win the war, soldiers needed to be—in the words of the military's sex education campaign—free from disease and fit to fight.[11] President Wilson himself, after all, had promised that men would come home only with scars they had won in war, meaning *not* venereal disease. Military and civilian officials believed that the "right kind" of women were key to keeping men from these twin evils.[12] Soldiers "must be furnished with healthful amusement," one warned, "or they will turn to . . . the first petticoat they see."[13]

The second goal was to add what the national commander of the Salvation Army, Evangeline Booth, called the "refining" influence of women to the military environment.[14] The American public not only feared for the moral safety of their sons, they also feared that a militarized, all-male environment would lead the men to abandon all sense of decorous behavior. In this context, women serving pie or listening sympathetically to a lonesome soldier brought a sense of family and domesticity to the Western Front that was designed to reassure the men's families that the military was not ruining their sons. Even more, officials insisted that socializing and dancing with American women in canteens and huts reminded men of their duty as soldiers to fight for the protection of women from home.

In both of these regards, women were key to making the AEF a more wholesome environment for the nation's sons. This work drew upon some of women's oldest wartime roles—to maintain the home fires and rear responsible citizens, but it relocated those duties to the war zone.[15] So, again, a bit of the old and a bit of the new.

If you think about these two tasks, though, they require two different kinds of women. To keep men away from prostitutes, you need women whom the men will see as viable alternatives. They were not to provide the same services as prostitutes—that was definitely *not* what the YMCA, Salvation Army, and military had in mind—but they were to be enticing enough to draw men into the canteens and recreation huts and away from the prostitutes who were readily available. At the same time, to domesticate the military, to make it more like a family, you needed women who could provide moral influence, women who would have a maternal influence over the doughboys. This meant that the organizations needed women who could fulfill many roles. They needed to be alluring but not too alluring. They needed to be friendly and welcoming but not too forward. They needed to be able to symbolize one young man's mother or sister but another man's sweetheart. It was a tough balance to strike for the organizations sending these women but especially for the women who had to be all of these things.

The women came from all over, and it's hard to say exactly how many of them were from the South. Generally, though, they were in their late twenties, single, native born, Protestant, from urban areas, and more educated than the average woman of the era. All but 3 of the 3,500 were white. About two-thirds of them had worked in education or a clerical job before the war, typical for women workers of the middle classes.

Women's work required them to be friendly and open to men with whom they would not have socialized before the war. The AEF included a high percentage of poor white southerners, while 18 percent of the soldiers had been born in a foreign country, not men who would have been in the women's social circles ordinarily.[16] Yet, many of the women embraced the chance to meet new people. Sometimes, the women were genuinely interested in the men's experiences; sometimes, the women viewed the men as a kind of cultural experiment but only for the war's duration.

This contrast in backgrounds between the women and the doughboys was exactly what the military and reform organizations intended. Nancy argued in her book on the CTCA that the point of recreation was to make men moral, which meant instilling in them middle-class values.[17] That goal extended to the AEF. One woman working with the YMCA explained that she and the other women had to make it clear to the men that their canteen was not "an east side bowery saloon" and that they had to behave "like gentlemen" to be served.[18]

So, in many ways, women's work echoed old ideas about women's wartime roles. As surrogate mothers, the women embodied the old idea that women should mother the nation's warriors who fought for them in return. But canteen work also took women to the war in these roles, and thus, the women had wartime experiences that few other women had. They embraced the dangers and the opportunities of the war, and they saw their work as the feminine equivalent of soldiering and a sign of their growing place in the nation.

RUTH SMITH TRUSS: My research is on the 167th Infantry Regiment, part of the 42nd Rainbow Division and as such a National Guard regiment.[19] The three other regiments in the 42nd Division were the 168th Iowa, the 165th New York, and the 166th Ohio. I'd say probably 90 percent of the membership of the 167th were Alabamians. That dropped a little bit throughout the war as they had replacements, but nevertheless we have a southern regiment mixed with midwestern and northern regiments.

So did the experience of these Alabamians replicate that of these other regiments? Well, the military, of course, is about uniformity; they literally *dress* in uniforms. So in many ways what the 167th experienced *was* the same. It didn't matter if they were from the South or the North or the Midwest. For an example of that, since we are on the campus of the University of Alabama, the surgeon general during World War I for the United States was William Crawford Gorgas. And if you're from Alabama and certainly if you're from this campus, you've heard the name Gorgas. He was an Alabamian, he was a southerner. His real claim to fame was cleaning up the Panama Canal Zone; he was a sanitarian. That was his background, his medical background, and so when the war began, he was ready. He had already studied the war's sanitary practices in Europe, he'd already looked at how they were organized there, and so he added the Sanitary Corps in 1917 as well as some other divisions within the medical department. So he had this group whose purpose was to focus on sanitation, who said, "OK, we're going to look at sanitation and then we'll let the medical folks actually do the treatment." So sanitation was one of the points that was emphasized in training. Again, this is just as true for southerners as for everyone else.

Once they were over there, two examples of how southerners' experiences were the same as others' concern wound treatment and body lice. Lice was an accepted and ubiquitous part of the World War I experiences of these men in France, wherever you were from and especially if you were fighting in trenches. When I was doing my dissertation research in the late 1980s, I talked with Henry Gaines Burnett, a World War I veteran; he said, "Well, yeah, what we used to do, we used to get you and your buddy, you'd each pick a louse, you know, get your best louse," and they would put them on the wall and have a race to see whose body louse was the fastest!

Another common experience would have been in the treatment of wounds. This veteran that I interviewed was actually wounded twice. The first time came in May 1918 when he was shot through the fleshy part of his calf; the round went in and out, and so he went immediately to the first aid station where there were these levels of medical care. He told me that the way they treated him initially was they took a piece of gauze, dipped it in iodine, and then strung a length of thread through the piece of gauze and then just pulled that piece of gauze through the hole in his leg. It sounds almost barbaric, but actually, I've asked some doctors who said that that was a pretty good and efficient method of getting some antiseptic in there and kind of cleaning out the wound. So this Alabamian was treated the same as, say, an Iowan who might have been wounded in much the same manner; everyone would have received the same type of medical treatment.

Conversely, however, similar circumstances did not necessarily lead to similar responses or reactions from southerners. I want to talk about how, in the opinion of contemporary observers, Alabamians reacted or responded differently from their fellow soldiers. They noted how differently the Alabamians in the 167th responded to certain circumstances compared with other troops. One way was that, apparently, the Alabamians complained less. They had a reputation for being able to bear pain better than their fellow soldiers. When they were wounded, they seemed to complain less about the pain. They complained less about the food. There was a dish that the men called "slum," and most everybody complained about how it tasted, how it was cold. The southerners, on the other hand, considered it "an appetizing and nourishing concoction of meat and vegetables"; so clearly, these southerners liked their food.

Another difference observers noted was the 167th's reputation—and it would depend on your point of view, how you would characterize this—as rambunctious, belligerent, aggressive, quick to take offense, competitive, and reckless. However you want to describe that trait, men of the 167th were identified as having a lot more of it than others. It depends on the situation whether or not those are good traits to have. In some cases, that competitiveness or willingness to engage in violence is worrisome and problematic. For example, these were the same men who were on the Mexican border, and they got into racial conflicts with the 10th Cavalry. This goes back to what Chad was saying—the commanders took care of that by splitting up the 10th Cavalry and moving them away from the Alabamians. Jennifer was talking about sectional reconciliation during World War I. Well, the men of the 167th didn't get that memo, at least not initially, because when they first joined the other regiments at Camp Mills in New York, they got in a fight with the men from New York, the 165th, so they were working through their reconciliation there.

But once they got to France, the men of the 167th became noted for their aggressiveness in patrolling and crossing no man's land. The men were known as the best in the 42nd Division certainly and some of the best on the Western Front at getting into no man's land, crossing over, and taking German prisoners of war.

An example of the 167th's different reaction to the same circumstances: when the Americans in the 42nd Division took over an entire divisional sector from the French, they thought they were doing it very stealthily. When they got there, the Germans had taken white sheets and printed on them so the men of the 42nd Division could see: "Welcome Rainbow Division," and the 42nd Division of course is the Rainbow Division. The New Yorkers treated the incident with a bit of trepidation, but the men of the 167th took it as a challenge and as an affront to Alabama's honor. Taking advantage of that patrol capacity they had, one night, men from the 167th took their own signs, crossed no man's land, and put up the signs on the wire facing the Germans. These signs read, "Germans, give your soul to God because your ass belongs to Alabam."

Perhaps unsurprisingly, then, at least according to their contemporaries, these Alabamians manifested a desire to fight unmatched by any other regiment within the Forty-Second Division. Certainly they paid for that, oftentimes with their casualties, but one general said—and this actually was from the Mexican border period—"In time of war, send me all the Alabamians you can get, but in time of peace, for Lord's sake, send them to somebody else." A member of the Forty-Second Division said, speaking of the men from Alabama, "'I do not know if they would make good parlor pets or proper chaperones for young ladies at the movies, but they sure are wonderful fighters.'"[20]

So if you can find a positive part of the rambunctiousness or belligerence, aggressiveness, and willingness to take on a challenge, then the men of the 167th were able to show that during the fight. Now outside of the fighting, yes, they certainly caused problems, but for the most part, they earned a reputation as great fighters during World War I, not just as the 167th but as part of the 42nd Division. After the war, documents recovered from the Germans suggest they found the 42nd Division one of the four best and toughest American divisions they faced in the war.

AUDIENCE: How were other people of color represented in the US Army during World War I, and how did they respond to foreign service? And were African American soldiers aware of the sort of more insidious colonial racism that existed in France? Were they commenting about it, or were they just sort of saying it was still better than the United States?

WILLIAMS: The army reflected the diversity of the country, but it also reflected the racialized nature of the country as well, particularly in terms of a very dichotomized black and white binary, as far as what race meant. You do have Native Americans serving in the American Expeditionary Forces, Latinos, whether from Puerto Rico or from the Southwest, but they were experiencing service in a country and military that conceived of race in very black and white terms. For example, many Puerto Ricans served in the Ninety-Second Division because they were seen as black, whereas Mexican Americans from the Southwest served in integrated units because they were seen, in the context of how race was constructed at this time, as white. So we see how race functions in different ways for different groups of people in the country.

To your second question, and this was one of the more eye-opening aspects of my research: I looked at the interactions between African American and African colonial troops hoping to find these moments of solidarity, of black soldiers saying, "Yes, you know, we're brothers and we share a common experience in terms of fighting American racism and you fighting against colonial oppression." And that really wasn't there. I mean you see some anecdotal evidence of that, mostly among African American troops who were more educated, who had the literacy and linguistic skills to be able to interact with their French counterparts. But by and large, you have African American soldiers who were internalizing and also replicating the same type of stereotypes that white Americans and French colonialists had of African troops. So their experiences really highlighted how different they were from their African counterparts, but how superior they were as well, how African Americans kind of saw themselves as having a higher level of civilization and development, particularly in terms of mastering the art of modern warfare more than the Tirailleurs Senegalais, who, for example, were used as shock troops and seen as savage fighters who were willing to risk their lives without any care in the world.

AUDIENCE: This question is for Dr. Williams. In *Torchbearers of Democracy*, you said that the experience of African American troops helped to launch the Harlem Renaissance. I was wondering if you could talk a little bit about that.

WILLIAMS: I would certainly make the argument that World War I and the experiences of African American troops were pivotal in launching the Harlem Renaissance or, to use a more expansive term, the New Negro Renaissance. Mark Whalan has written a really good book on the culture of the New Negro and he specifically connects it to World War I, looking at a number of the key artists of the Harlem Renaissance who invoke the war in their various forms of artistry—plays, poems, artwork, even movies, someone like Oscar Micheaux for example.[21] The war was really pivotal as a cultural moment and kind of pushes back against the idea that African Americans didn't want anything to do with memories of the war, that they were somehow so painful and traumatic that they just wanted to forget about them.

I argue that that wasn't the case. The Harlem Renaissance and cultural production during that period speaks to just how significant the war was as a moment. You have a number of black veterans who were active participants in the Harlem Renaissance in different ways, whether as musicians or artists. But also thinking about what that means politically as well and making sure not to disassociate the cultural from the political when we talk about the New Negro Renaissance, you have black veterans who were engaged in various forms of political activism. This was certainly happening in the North. Mike brought up the role of the Great Migration in transforming the cultural and political dynamics of urban areas, whether New York or Chicago or other places. But it also affected urban areas in the South and spurred specific movements. The Universal Negro Improvement Association, for example, is oftentimes explicitly associated with the North, but it had chapters throughout the South, and I suspect that there were a number of former veterans who were active in the UNIA in its different localities. So yes, I think it is really important to acknowledge the whole range of different experiences but also to think about the everyday forms of resistance as well and take them seriously at the level of political consciousness.

AUDIENCE: For Dr. Truss, did the 167th Alabama really have Bowie knives that they brought to battle with them? And Dr. Williams, could you speak more to how exactly the military thought racial segregation would aid military efficiency?

TRUSS: According to Rod Frazer's book, *Send the Alabamians*, the men were issued "trench knives," which had a metal knuckle guard and little utilitarian value.[22]

WILLIAMS: If you look at War Department documents and the records of the American Expeditionary Forces, officials were extremely concerned about racial friction, about what could happen when black and white soldiers interacted with one another, about the possibly inevitable result being an all-out race riot. And certainly the Houston Rebellion, as I term it, of August 1917, was kind of the perfect example of the fears that existed, particularly among white southerners, but also within the hierarchy of the War Department and the army as a whole.[23] So segregation was seen as a method of efficiency in trying to keep black and white soldiers apart in order to have a functional army that was not going to devolve into all-out racial turmoil. And that was certainly the case overseas as well.

But at the same time, it's also important to remember that the color line was always very fluid. As hard as the military tried to institute a strict policy of segregation, it was always breaking down in different ways. You do have instances where black and white soldiers were interacting with each other. Sometimes those interactions were incredibly violent; other times they were not. But as a policy, segregation—and Jim Crow as it was couched by progressives of the time—was seen as a method of efficiency in maintaining cordial and peaceful race relations.

AUDIENCE: Was there any evidence of white soldiers understanding this contradiction between fighting a war for democracy and yet fighting in this incredibly segregated system? Did they talk about that at all in 1917, 1918, or were they living in a cognitive dissonance that just couldn't be pierced?

TRUSS: Yes, the latter.

WILLIAMS: You're referring to white southerners?

AUDIENCE: Yes. I understand that black southerners saw the contradiction.

WILLIAMS: Yes. Certainly you see some northern white officers commanding black troops were kind of aware of this inconsistency between the ideals that the United States was fighting for and the reality, men who at times develop great sympathy for the men under their command. But I think by and large white southerners saw no contradiction. If anything, the war kind of reinforced the need for them to hold on to those kind of white supremacist ideals and to enforce them as strongly as possible because they were well aware of what the consequences could be after the war.

AUDIENCE: My question is for you, Dr. Williams. I'm wondering if you can speak to the experience of African American women. What impact did their gender have on how they experienced the war?

WILLIAMS: One of the best books on the black experience in the war is titled *Two Colored Women in the AEF*, written by Kathryn Johnson and Addie Hunton, and they were two of only three black women who served with the YMCA overseas.[24] They were responsible for providing services within the segregated structure of the YMCA to those two hundred thousand black soldiers who served overseas. It was a wholly unrealistic task but one that they internalized and took very seriously. It really speaks to the particular kind of racial and gendered consciousness of black women during the war who internalized a kind of racial motherhood, if you will. They saw it as their responsibility to care for these men and they faced incredibly difficult situations, but I think it was also incredibly important in terms of their broadened racial and gendered consciousness, kind of the emergence of a New Negro womanhood as an important development of the war both domestically and internationally as well. Kathryn Johnson, for example, attended the Pan African Congress in 1919. These were women who were very politically active, very internationally conscious as well.[25]

VUIC: I would echo Chad's comments. Johnson and Hunton saw their work for the YMCA as especially necessary because of segregation, because black soldiers were treated so poorly, and they saw themselves as embodying a particular image of black womanhood for those men. They very much internalized the YMCA's goal of having women symbolize the home and family in an effort to keep those men on the straight and narrow. They spoke about the food they served as being meaningful to the men because it reminded them of their mothers' cooking. They also categorized themselves as mothers in part to offer the men's families at home a reassuring image. They insisted that despite the expansive experiences the men were having in French society and, in particular, with French women, the men all just wanted to return home, to return to American women back home. In that sense, they saw themselves as representing the nation—which was what the YMCA and Salvation Army wanted all women to symbolize—and in the years after the war, Johnson in particular claimed this symbolic work as proof that she'd done her job as a citizen in the war. After having done her part in the war, she sailed home on a segregated ship, which reinforced for her the failure of the war for democracy. Her wartime experiences strengthened a commitment to racial equality that she'd had from a young age. A few years after the war, she put on her YMCA uniform and a sandwich board to protest a screening of the film *Birth of a Nation*. She'd represented America in France, her sign protested, and she refused to let the racist film represent her in the United States. For her, her work in a YMCA canteen had fulfilled her wartime obligation as a citizen, and she demanded equal treatment in return.[26]

AUDIENCE: I have a question or a plea for distinction on some terminology for Dr. Williams. You used the terms "white supremacy" and "racial discrimination." I grew up as a southerner the first twenty-five years of my life in a segregated society, so that's my reality. I would classify most southerners as believing in the concept of separate but equal as opposed to white "supremacy." I'm just wondering what your experience is with this and whether you make that kind of distinction as you view the morality of attitudes past.

WILLIAMS: I use the term "white supremacy" very deliberately. We are talking about a set of practices, a set of ideas, that is thoroughly ingrained and institutionalized throughout the US military and comes directly out of the particular history and social and political realities of black life in the South. So I understand sensitivity to that term, especially nowadays, but it's real, and I think it aptly characterizes the nature of the military in the context of World War I and perhaps aptly characterizes the nature of the American nation as a whole. You can certainly point to how that manifests itself in different forms of racial discrimination and how it gets internalized in different ways by white soldiers. White southerners practiced white supremacy in different ways, but I do think white supremacy served as a unifying principle. If we're talking about the South, about what white southerners have in common with one another, I do think we need to take that seriously. We need to really reckon with it in ways that I think historians still haven't fully done, recognizing that yes, there are important differences between different types of white southerners and the way that they practiced race and their own racial identity. But what did it mean for them to live in a society that was so driven by these ideas of white supremacy? I think it's important to reckon with that question.

VUIC: You see this commitment to white supremacy in recreation as well, and it's something that is deliberately enforced. It's not something that just happened. The YMCA and the military contributed to racial segregation in the war by segregating recreation huts. On occasion, a hut served both white and black soldiers, but in those cases military officers quickly reversed the integration and enforced segregation. Black and white men couldn't even eat donuts together. The white women who served the segregated donuts accepted the practice. Kathryn Johnson and Addie Hunton, the two

African American women Chad mentioned who worked with the YMCA in France, noted in their book that white women's prejudices prevented them from truly helping African American men. Because the YMCA only sent three black women to France, white women sometimes served coffee and donuts to black troops. But, as Johnson and Hunton observed, the white women didn't offer the same kind of care and sympathy for the black men as they did for white men.

Their resistance to working with black troops reveals how much they were committed to racial divides when we consider that these women were willing to cross other social divisions, including class and ethnicity. We often think of young people as being more open-minded than their parents, and many of the women saw the war as an opportunity for them to mingle with people they never would have met or associated with before the war. One young woman, for example, took great pleasure in telling her parents that she had become friends with an Irish boxer. She almost taunted them with the idea that she was associating with a man her parents would have thought well below their social class and they couldn't do anything about it. A lot of women really enjoyed meeting immigrant men and those from different parts of the country. But women, even women who considered themselves open-minded and progressive on many social and cultural issues, were not willing to cross the color line that was becoming more and more entrenched in American society.

TRUSS: I'd just add that we've talked a lot about the progressives, about the Progressive Era, but to comprehend this idea of racial strife, especially across the South, we really have to go back to the Populist Era. In Alabama, we have the 1901 constitution. How did we get there? We have to understand the division that was fostered among poor whites and blacks as a result of the Populist Era as important background to the Great War period.

AUDIENCE: May I add something to that, please? I haven't done as much research as Dr. Williams has on this particular issue, but I have researched race relations in the World War I era. White southerners fully admit, explicitly, that they are white supremacists in the documents.

AUDIENCE: In *Send the Alabamians*, Nimrod Frazer wrote that local newspapers in Alabama regarded the 167th as the "Immortals," but I just wonder why did the newspapers give them that nickname and where did the nickname come from? And what factors impacted the cohesion and combat performance of the 167th on the battlefield?

TRUSS: In 1919 regimental chronicler William Amerine used the term.[27] Whether he was the first to use it or whether it was a newspaper editor, I don't know. The French called them *les tigres* because of their ferociousness in battle. In terms of cohesiveness, that's one thing that makes the 167th different from the heavily drafted army we've talked about here. These men were primarily volunteers. They were already in the National Guard, and so they had basically self-selected into the military. Many of them were very well educated, especially compared to the average Alabamian. Some of the speakers today have talked about poor and rural men who were drafted and who opposed the draft. That's certainly true in some cases, but not for many of these men. They were dedicated, by and large loyal, and they were more professional. That's one thing that the Defense Act of 1916 did; it helped to professionalize the National Guard. So they were not just plucked from the farm. They had been, since 1916, in service with the regular army on the Mexican border, and so they had lived under all the rules and regulations; they were accustomed to that life, much more so than just a regular draftee would have been. I think they were different in that sense; plus they had trained together, worked together, and so they did have that sort of cohesiveness. That dynamic applied more to the men of the 167th than to a drafted Alabamian assigned to something like the 82nd Division.

JENNIFER KEENE (FROM AUDIENCE): I just wanted to weigh in on the question of racial prejudice and white supremacy. I've read lots of soldiers' letters in the First World War, and I think it's interesting that you can clearly see people buying into a concept of white supremacy even in the absence of overt racial language or racial slurs. One example: it was common for soldiers complaining about manual work or a job they felt was demeaning to say things like, "This is no way to treat a white man." It's very common to see soldiers who believed military service would bring them upward social mobility, whether through sending money home and creating savings accounts or through buying federal bonds or investment insurance, to say things like, "After the war, we'll be able to live like a white man should." To me, many working-class whites were holding onto a white identity they regarded as tenuous. They weren't railing against African American soldiers, there was nothing overtly racist in their commentary, but they were clearly influenced by a society in which whiteness meant something. The feeling that they were not being treated as white suggests that they were not being given the elevated status that they deserved because of their skin color. So I think that it's an ideological framework in which white supremacy was omnipresent in how people perceived the world. You don't have to find racial language to see it working. Sorry, not a question.

WILLIAMS: No, amen.

AUDIENCE: Jennifer was talking earlier about the American army in World War I as a melting pot, which in many respects was certainly the case. But as it's conceived originally, the army had a strong regional focus. When people talk about African American units in World War I, they tend to focus on the 369th out of Harlem and they might talk less about the other units in the 93rd Division such as the National Guard unit out of Chicago and so forth. Just for informational purposes for those of us interested in World War I who want to look at a group of black southerners who served together, where do we look? I've heard that the 366th in the 92nd Division had a large contingent of Alabama men, and I'm wondering if you can give us any other examples where there are pioneer regiments where most of the men in that outfit came from a particular locality.

WILLIAMS: Yeah, it's a good question. I mean you certainly do see examples within the 92nd Division. You mentioned the 366th. The 367th Infantry Regiment in the 92nd Division if I'm not mistaken was largely from New York. So you do have kind of similar practices of raising units according to locality. I believe you do see some of that manifested in various labor battalions as well, certainly just as a matter of convenience. I mentioned the importance of looking at the stateside experiences. Most of these men were used for labor capacities, building camps, so it was essential to get men to work as quickly as possible. So you do see some of those kinds of regional identities being solidified and coalescing, but at the same time, you see really interesting interactions between men from different parts of the country and the world as well.

NANCY BRISTOW (FROM AUDIENCE): I want to add a quick comment and then a question for Chad. I also use the term "white supremacy" when talking about the situation for African American soldiers during the war, and I'll add one other piece to it. I wrote a book on recreation programs for soldiers that tried to keep them both morally and physically fit for service by training them to new sensibilities.[28] In those programs, there were recreational facilities, run by the YWCA and YMCA, to which men could go to write letters and have appropriately controlled social time with women. Almost universally such spaces were absolutely segregated and thus completely unequal. Soldiers lived in this white supremacist context, and white soldiers, including officers, generally found it not only acceptable but preferable. And so for me, the language of "white supremacy" is necessary to foreground that historical reality.

But I had a follow-up question for you, Chad. You talked about sexualized stereotypes of the African American soldier. Is there an appropriate connection to be made to the postwar practices of lynching and violence against soldiers returning home?

WILLIAMS: Oh yeah, absolutely. As I said, Vardaman can be used anecdotally, but these were fears that were rampant throughout the South. When black soldiers, who had been overseas interacting with and having sex with French women, returned home, would they think that it was OK to have sex with a southern white woman? These kinds of historic sexualized anxieties and fears around black men went back all the way to the antebellum period but now got modernized in the context of World War I and focused on the bodies of returned black veterans. So we see a lot of racial violence after the war. The number of lynchings spiked to I believe seventy-six in 1919. You have a number of black veterans who were lynched in uniform for various reasons. But the sexual subtext was always there, even if black men knew the reasons why they were assaulted or in the most brutal cases lynched had nothing to do with their interactions with a white woman. That was always the rationale that was given—keeping the South safe for white womanhood.[29]

NOTES

1. Scholars have yet to fully employ "the South" as an interpretative framework in exploring the experiences of black soldiers and their regional diversity. Several works, however, do address various aspects of southern black soldiers' unique experiences and identities. They include Arthur E. Barbeau and Florette Henri, *The Unknown Soldiers: African-American Troops in World War I* (Philadelphia: Temple University Press, 1974); Jeanette Keith, *Rich Man's War, Poor Man's Fight: Race, Class and Power in the Rural South during the First World War* (Chapel Hill: University of North Carolina Press, 2004); Jennifer D. Keene, *Doughboys, the Great War, and the Remaking of America* (Baltimore: Johns Hopkins University Press, 2001); Adriane Lentz-Smith, *Freedom Struggles: African Americans and World War I* (Cambridge, MA: Harvard University Press, 2009); Nina Mjagkij, *Loyalty in Time of Trial: The African American Experience during World War I* (Lanham, MD: Rowman and Littlefield, 2011); Chad L. Williams, *Torchbearers of Democracy: African American Soldiers in the World War I Era* (Chapel Hill: University of North Carolina Press, 2010).

2. Rayford Whittingham Logan, *The Betrayal of the Negro, from Rutherford B. Hayes to Woodrow Wilson* (New York: Collier Books, 1965). Also see Keith Robert Janken, *Rayford W. Logan and the Dilemma of the African-American Intellectual* (Amherst: University of Massachusetts Press, 1993).

3. W. E. B. Du Bois, "The African Roots of War," *Atlantic Monthly*, May 1915, 707–14.

4. See Williams, *Torchbearers of Democracy*, chap. 4.

5. See Jennifer D. Keene, "French and American Racial Stereotypes during the First World War," in *National Stereotypes in Perspective: Americans in France, Frenchmen in America*, ed. William Chew (Amsterdam: Rodopi, 2001), 261–81.

6. Robert Lee Bullard, *Personalities and Reminiscences of the War* (Garden City, NY: Doubleday, Page, 1925).

7. Elizabeth Cobbs, *The Hello Girls: America's First Women Soldiers* (Cambridge, MA: Harvard University Press, 2017); Lynn Dumenil, *The Second Line of Defense: American Women and World War I* (Chapel Hill: The University of North Carolina Press, 2017); Jean Ebbert and Marie-Beth Hall, *The First, The Few, The Forgotten: Navy and Marine Corps Women in World War I* (Annapolis, MD: Naval Institute Press, 2002); Lettie Gavin, *American Women in World War I: They Also Served* (Boulder: University Press of Colorado, 1997); Kimberley Jensen, *Mobilizing Minerva: American Women in the First World War* (Urbana: University of Illinois Press, 2008); Susan Zeiger, *In Uncle Sam's Service: Women Workers with the American Expeditionary Force, 1917–1919* (Ithaca, NY: Cornell University Press, 1999).

8. Kara Dixon Vuic, *The Girls Next Door: Bringing the Home Front to the Front Lines* (Cambridge, MA: Harvard University Press, 2019).

9. Keith, *Rich Man's War, Poor Man's Fight*.

10. Nancy K. Bristow, *Making Men Moral: Social Engineering during the Great War* (New York: New York University Press, 1996).

11. *Keeping Fit to Fight* was the title of a pamphlet and, later, a film, prepared by the American Social Hygiene Association and distributed widely among AEF forces, which warned doughboys of the dangers of sexual activity.

12. Luther H. Gulick, *Morals and Morale* (New York: Association Press, 1919), 3.

13. "Her Share in War," *NYT Magazine*, June 2, 1918.

14. "Why the Salvation Army Is at the Front," *War Service Herald* 8, no. 1 (January 1918): 15.

15. In the United States, this notion took shape during the Revolutionary period in particular. Historian Linda K. Kerber termed it "Republican Motherhood." See *Women of the Republic: Intellect and Ideology in Revolutionary America* (Chapel Hill: University of North Carolina Press, 1980), especially chap. 2.

16. Keene, *Doughboys*, 20; Jennifer D. Keene, *World War I*, Daily Life through History Series (Greenwood, CT.: Greenwood Press, 2006), 37.

17. Bristow, *Making Men Moral*.

18. Gertrude Bray Diary, 38 and 51, Gertrude Bray, YMCA, World War I Veterans Survey Collection, Military History Institute, Army Heritage and Education Center, Carlisle, PA.

19. See Ruth Smith Truss, "The Alabama National Guard at Home and Abroad, 1914–1919" in *The Great War in the Heart of Dixie: Alabama in World War I*, ed. Martin

Olliff (Tuscaloosa: University of Alabama Press, 2008), 24–40; Truss, "The Alabama National Guard's 167th Infantry Regiment in World War I," *Alabama Review* 56 (January 2003): 3–34; Truss, "Progress toward Professionalism: The Alabama National Guard on the Mexican Border, 1916–1917," *Military History of the West* 30 (Fall 2000): 97–121; Truss, "Alabama National Guard," "167th Infantry Regiment," and "William Preston Screws" articles in *Encyclopedia of Alabama*, www.encyclopediaofalabama.org; Truss, "The Alabama National Guard, 1900–1920," PhD dissertation, University of Alabama, 1992.

20. The preceding examples come from James J. Cooke, *The Rainbow Division in the Great War, 1917–1919* (Westport, CT: Praeger), 61, 63, 80, 179. Other examples—from a *Collier's Weekly* correspondent and from Father Francis P. Duffy, chaplain of New York's 165th—are found in Nimrod T. Frazer, *Send the Alabamians: World War I Fighters in the Rainbow Division* (Tuscaloosa: University of Alabama Press, 2014), 204.

21. Mark Whalan, *The Great War and the Culture of the New Negro* (Gainesville: University Press of Florida, 2008).

22. Frazer, *Send the Alabamians*, 40.

23. See Robert V. Haynes, *A Night of Violence: The Houston Riot of 1917* (Baton Rouge: Louisiana State University Press, 1976); Lentz-Smith, *Freedom Struggles*; Tyina L. Steptoe, *Houston Bound: Culture and Color in a Jim Crow City* (Berkeley: University of California Press, 2015), 31–35; Williams, *Torchbearers of Democracy*.

24. Addie W. Hunton and Kathryn M. Johnson, *Two Colored Women with the A.E.F.* (New York: G. K. Hall, 1920).

25. Also see Nikki Brown, *Private Politics and Public Voices: Black Women's Activism from World War I to the New Deal* (Bloomington: Indiana University Press, 2006).

26. Hunton and Johnson, *Two Colored Women with the A. E. F.*

27. *Alabama's Own in France* (New York: Eaton and Gettinger, 1919), 10.

28. Bristow, *Making Men Moral*.

29. See Williams, *Torchbearers of Democracy*, chap. 6.

4

Finding Meaning in the Great War

Jonathan H. Ebel, Derryn Moten, and Steven Trout

The end of the First World War triggered the start of a different type of conflict, one centered on the public meaning of the conflict. Jonathan Ebel, Derryn Moten, and Steven Trout directed the conversation to the different and sometimes contradictory ways southerners came to understand and memorialize the Great War. Once again, race played a central role in the discussion, as the panelists surveyed how white and black Americans experienced and remembered the war differently. Moten specifically asked listeners to consider the role of historically black colleges and universities in training the corps of black officers and in turn inspiring and preparing many for leadership in later civil rights struggles. Members of the audience raised important questions about the meaning of southern civil religion, the relationship of black educational institutions to the production of black memory, the place of black writers in the formation of a southern literary response to the war, and the tradition of marine veterans turning to literature to come to terms with combat experience.

JONATHAN EBEL: I'm trained in the history of Christianity and American religious history, and I was drawn initially to the study of religion and war. In the last five or so years, it occurred to me that a lot of the scholarship on religion and war in America felt like a way that we could continue to talk about the agency of white men without apologizing for focusing on white men and their agency. We were focusing on killing, cruelty, suffering, industrialized violence, premature death, and other things that morally sound people find troubling. We were asking important questions about justifications, theodicy, moral frameworks, and the violation thereof. But the actors in these tragedies—and more often than not the tragic heroes—were white men. Somehow the fact that they were crying out to God for deliverance from the consequences of war, that they died young or were forever scarred, obscured the continued, relentless centering of white men in this inquiry.

And so I've moved away from more traditional ways of thinking about religion and war toward the topic of my last book, which was civil religion, and the project that I'm working on the side, a religious history of American weaponry. The religious history of the hand grenade is one that I've been developing over the last couple of years. I won't be saying a whole lot today about clergy or about institutional churches. I'm happy to answer questions about them, but really what I want to talk about is civil religion and a couple of varieties of civil religion: the nationalist variety that many people have written on, and the distinct but related phenomenon of civil religion in the American South. And when I say civil religion, what I mean is symbols, rituals, institutions, and narratives that orient people in history and give them a sense of purpose. Scholars, as I mentioned, have long noted the presence of two strains of civil religion in America: the nationalist strain and this southern strain famously associated with the Civil War and the religion of the Lost Cause. I'm interested in the interplay between these two in the Great War, how they occupied not just the same civic sphere but sometimes the same human bodies. To be specific, by "the American South," I actually mean three particular southerners: Kiffin Rockwell of Tennessee and South Carolina, Felicita Hecht of Virginia, and James Favors of Florida. These three subjects give us three distinct perspectives on the evolving phenomenon of civil religion in the Great War era and help highlight some of the problems with that phenomenon as practiced and as conceptualized.

So first, Kiffin Rockwell. Rockwell was born in Newport, Tennessee, in 1892. His father, James, a Baptist preacher, died when he was young. Kiffin subsequently attended primary and secondary school in North Carolina.[1] From his earliest days, he lived, moved, and had his being in southern civil religion. His grandfathers told stories of their exploits as Confederate officers, witnesses to the Civil War, the Ur event of southern civil religion. He attended Virginia Military Institute and Washington and Lee, two institutions dedicated to cultivating southern gentlemen and southern honor. Kiffin is the Dixie Doughboy par excellence, except for the fact that he wasn't ever a doughboy. Kiffin and his brother Paul decamped for France in August 1914 and joined the French Foreign Legion. After recovering from a leg wound, Kiffin became a pilot with the Lafayette Escadrille. In June 1915, he wrote to his mother, "So, if I should be killed, I think you ought to be proud in knowing that your son tried to be a man and was not afraid to die, and that he gave his life for a greater cause than most people do: the cause of humanity. Otherwise, I may never do anything worthwhile or any good to anyone after the war and may live to regret that I wasn't killed in it."[2]

This wealthy white young man moved easily from his southernness to global citizenship and sacrifice, focusing on the irreducible meaning of a soldier's death and the resonance of dying for a cause. Rockwell was dead long before the first soldier of the American Expeditionary Force [AEF] set foot on French soil. His eyes never settled on the *Stars and Stripes*, the weekly newspaper published by the AEF for its soldiers in France. But had he seen that paper, he would surely have felt the force of America's nationalist strain of civil religion, from illustrations featuring a somber, sainted Abraham Lincoln to regular articles that connected the heroics of Union armies and those of the American Expeditionary Force. Southern identity and southern civil religion, traditions that shaped the identities of Kiffin and Paul Rockwell and hundreds of thousands of other soldiers from the South, were things to get over in the name of national unity.

As I see it, the regular vigorous presentation of a united United States betrays a concern for fractiousness and national woundedness—a work that the nationalist civil religion still had to accomplish. Southern civil religion was one, but not the only, divisive force. Indeed, one of the more interesting documents I've encountered in studying the war is a crude map of Europe created by the American Battle Monuments Commission [ABMC]. The map is full of dots marking the European locales where recently immigrated families chose to bury sons who had given their lives for America. Italy and Ireland loomed large. Norway, Sweden, Poland are also sites of lots of little dots. Divided loyalties such as these had little place in the *Stars and Stripes* and had no place at all in the overseas military cemeteries designed and built by the ABMC. These memorial spaces emphasize unity, uniformity, shared purpose, shared sacrifice. Of course, divisions are present in those cemeteries anyway. Divisions that complicate nationalist civil religion and southern civil religion, which also, to be fair, papers over differences in service of a myth of the united South.

Felicita Hecht lived most of her life in Virginia. She worked as a private nurse around Norfolk. She was Catholic, and she was a widowed mother. When she transitioned into military service and prepared to deploy, she placed her two children in the care of a nun who ran a Catholic school. What Hecht did not know when she sailed for France on November 14, 1918, was that a malignant tumor was growing in her breast and that the disease had already metastasized to her lungs. She died in February 1919 after a few short months tending to the wounded. I haven't been able to learn anything about her orphaned children. I've thought a lot about Felicita Hecht, though. To me, her story underscores the gendered nature of civil religion, whether national or southern. The sacrifices these societies recognize and sanctify most readily are the blaze-of-glory type made by Kiffin Rockwell, not the mother dying an ocean away type made by Felicita and her children. I'm also fascinated by how completely obscured Felicita is by the place where her remains lie: Oise-Aisne American Cemetery in France. If we don't work to see the specifics of her life and death, we cannot appreciate the extent to which both were co-opted by civil religious discourses and structures. Put differently, when Americans take in Oise-Aisne cemetery and the six-thousand-plus crosses that fill the meticulously landscaped grave areas and imagine those buried there, we think first of men, likely white, who "laid down their lives" for friends, for nation, for freedom.

A few years ago, a friend passed me a document that I'm pretty sure we were not supposed to see. Perhaps someone else here has come across it in their research. I haven't incorporated it into my writing or talked about it publicly before. Its title is "Statement Concerning Capital Sentences Adjudged by General Courts-Martial against Members of the American Expeditionary Force in France and Carried into Execution." The document consists of three pages describing eleven executions of American soldiers. Ten of the eleven cases involved alleged rape or attempted rape. At least nine of those executed were African American.

I would like to read you one case. "Private James Favors, 331st Labor Battalion was convicted of rape. The victim was a French woman, thirty-eight years old. In the accomplishment of his purpose, Private Favors threw her to the ground, strangled her, kicked her, and bruised her face and arms. The offense was committed on August 15th, 1918. Private Favors was executed near Belville on November 8th, 1918." History doesn't give us much on Private Favors. He entered service from Florida. He had an allegedly violent sexual encounter with a French woman. He is now buried in Meuse-Argonne American Cemetery with roughly fourteen thousand other American soldiers and war workers. We can read this account superficially and be done. A rapist caught and convicted. He probably got what he deserved. We can also read it in light of the racial hierarchy so often associated with southern civil religion and the challenge to that hierarchy provided by France's literal and figurative embrace of the African American soldier and the ample evidence of systematic American efforts to reassert racial hierarchy. That nine of the eleven men executed for capital offenses were African American in an army in which African Americans constituted roughly 10 percent of personnel says more about the portability of Jim Crow and the racism of American justice than it says about those who committed such heinous crimes.

But what does it say about southern civil religion and American civil religion as practiced and described in the Great War? Civil religion was as racially coded as denominational affiliation. The AEF's leadership and America more broadly felt it important to attack the black soldier, a man who in and beyond war could lay claim to the stature and authority of military experience. I am also intrigued, though, that James Favors, Charles Chambers, William Buckner, Joe Cathy, and either William Henry or Sercey Strong (the report is unclear), all African American, all executed for similar crimes, are all buried in the hallowed grounds of American military cemeteries. Some might see their presence as a pollutant. American soldiers executed during World War II were buried separately. But I take it as an entirely proper, if unintentional, challenge to the mythology of war, to its imagined redemptive power, and to the rigid, often self-serving separation of nationalist civil religion from its coemergent southern equivalent.

DERRYN MOTEN: For those of you in the room who may not know this, Alabama State University [ASU] is one of two historically black public universities in the state of Alabama. Friends of mine back home in Indiana sometimes assume Alabama State is akin to Indiana State University, a PWI [predominantly white institution]. They're not the same. Alabama State University has celebrated its sesquicentennial, and the previous president, Dr. Gwendolyn Boyd, charged the history faculty to write the 150-year history of the university. And so we decided we would add to the university's best-known historical moment, the Montgomery Bus Boycott from December 1955 to January 1956, and try to find other significant historical moments in our history over the last century and a half. And so we combed through reels and reels of microfilm looking for this history, and much to our delight, we discovered that the university had a significant history in World War I, and that's what I'm going to talk about. We discovered that we had five graduates of the State Normal School at Montgomery— we weren't a college or a university then—who graduated from Fort Des Moines Negro Officers Training School in Des Moines, Iowa.

I can't tell you how excited I was when I learned this. I attended graduate school at the University of Iowa, so I knew something about the Fort Des Moines Negro Officers School. This school came about as a result of efforts by the NAACP and Howard University who lobbied the War Department. It was controversial. People argued that the NAACP should not push for a segregated school. But nevertheless, the NAACP, Howard, and other HBCU [historically black colleges and universities] presidents lobbied for the officers' school. The school opened in June 1917 and graduated its only class in October 1917. There were 639 graduates, and our normal school had five of those 639: William H. Benson, Clarence K. Howard, Charles H. Love, James H. Peyton, and Victor J. Tulane. These five were all members of the 366th Infantry within the American Expeditionary Forces, AEF, a unit described in a *Montgomery Advertiser* editorial "as Alabama's own colored regiment." We once had a William H. Benson men's residence hall. After the war, Benson moved to Chicago, becoming a prominent dentist and generous donor to our school. That's how I discovered that we had these five graduates of the Fort Des Moines Negro Officers School. These guys were the crème de la crème of black folks. They were the black intelligentsia, and this is not hyperbole. These men were literally recruited and handpicked by HBCU presidents on their campuses; they were professors, they were students; and they were the best of the best. And out of this graduating class, we had Lt. Charles Hamilton Houston.

Houston went on to become the associate dean of Howard University School of Law. He trained Thurgood Marshall and others. We also have Robert Abbott who founded the *Chicago Defender* newspaper. These men, to Chad's point in the last session, did in war what they would do as peace time civilians. They became part of the black leadership agitating for rights for African Americans in particular and all people in general. I also want to underscore what Chad said about black people linking service, either as civilians or soldiers, to citizenship and thought of themselves as citizens even if the US government did not. I encourage students in the room to read the letters of the soldiers in World War I, and I recommend the letters found in the papers of W. E. B. Du Bois. One gets a sense of how these men felt about fighting a war to make the world safe for democracy. Many of these black soldiers were fighting to make democracy real in Alabama.

So we have soldiers from the Fort Des Moines Negro Officers Training School that were part of our campus. In my research, I learned of the work of two other significant Alabamians. Emmet Jay Scott served eighteen years as personal secretary for Booker T. Washington until the latter's death in 1915. In October 1917, Secretary of War Newton D. Baker appointed Scott as special assistant to the secretary of war for black troops. Tuskegee, not the US government, paid Scott's salary. This turn of events did not come about by happenstance. Before Booker T. Washington's death, Robert Russa Moton and Tuskegee board member Julius Rosenwald attended a meeting in Washington, DC, concerning World War I where Scott's name was put forward. Moton succeeded Washington as principal of Tuskegee Institute and Normal School. Alabama governor Charles Henderson appointed Moton head of the Negro Committee of the Council of Defense. And Moton, like W. E. B. Du Bois, was sent to France to investigate the treatment of black soldiers in the AEF.

I first became interested in World War I when in graduate school, and I learned about a military execution that happened in Iowa on July 5, 1918. There, three black draftees from Alabama, Fred Allen of Georgiana, Robert Johnson of Sheffield, and Stanley Tramble of Roanoke, were hanged after their courts-martial for the rape of a seventeen-year-old white girl from Des Moines, Iowa. And unlike the executions in Houston in 1917 involving the Twenty-Fourth Infantry, the three Alabama soldiers had their court-martial records and their death sentences sent to Washington, DC, and Pres. Woodrow Wilson approved the death penalties for the trio. The three soldiers were hanged simultaneously. All black soldiers stationed at Camp Dodge were ordered to assemble at the parade grounds to witness the execution. The condemned died of asphyxiation with one soldier taking nearly an hour to die, giving credence that the condemned is to "hang by the neck until dead." Black soldiers had to stand at attention with their eyes fixed straight ahead. The hanging was to be an "object lesson" for the crime of rape and the racial taboo of interracial sex. "Negroes Executed for Black Crimes in 'Far Up' Iowa" headlined the July 5, 1918, *Columbus [Georgia] Ledger Enquirer*.

Following the war, Congress held hearings about the miscarriages of justice in military executions. Chief among the critics was Oregon's US senator George Chamberlain, chairman of the Senate Committee on Military Affairs. The senator did not mince words: "The records of courts-martial in this war show that we have no military law or system of administering military justice which is worthy of the name law or justice."[3] The US Army hanged twenty-four black soldiers during World War I on American soil, more than any other racial or ethnic group of US soldiers, and all but three were executed in Texas—members of the Twenty-Fourth Infantry.[4] The remaining three were the Alabama draftees hanged at Camp Dodge, Iowa.

Going back to the State Normal School at Montgomery, we discovered that faculty, students, and staff assisted community residents in starting or maintaining war gardens. The *Montgomery Advertiser* credited them with the creation of fourteen hundred gardens. Other faculty members assisted with war kitchens or war demonstration kitchens. There were kitchens in Birmingham, Montgomery, and Mobile. Montgomery's demonstration kitchen was located on the second floor of the A. Nachman Store on South Perry and Dexter Avenue. White women received cooking demonstrations on Tuesdays and Thursdays with black women receiving cooking demonstrations on Wednesdays. Laura Daly, the black home demonstration agent for the city of Montgomery and Montgomery County, worked at Tuskegee Institute but graduated from Hampton Institute. War kitchens showed women how to prepare meals substituting corn flour for wheat and prepare meals without meat. These demonstrations also included home economics advising women on the merits of keeping healthy and orderly homes. But there was tremendous interest in having black women attend these cooking demonstrations since many black women worked and cooked in white homes and since there was a belief that a frugal cook fostered a frugal nation.

Thrift was a theme emphasized in a July 4, 1918, festival that took place on the campus of State Normal School at Montgomery. The day began with segregated Independence Day parades in downtown Montgomery with the black parade spilling into Hornet Stadium. Under the banner, "Food Is as Necessary as Ammunition," there were speeches given by Four Minute Men, there were athletic events, and there was food including camp stew.

The activities of the State Normal School in Montgomery were not at all unique. Similar activities took place at Bennett College, a historically black school in Columbia, South Carolina, and at North Carolina A&T in Greensboro, a land grant HBCU. And I suspect events such as the ones previously mentioned happened in black communities across the nation, particularly those communities situated near a black college or university. What these stories tell us is that black people were patriotic and saw their sacrifices as vital to the successful outcome of the Great War. What we know is that loyalty and allegiance to the American flag did not eradicate or suspend Jim Crow. The immutability of white racism spawned the NAACP, gave birth to the New Negro, and Negritude, and ushered in a black militancy that sparked the modern civil rights movement. Essentially, I think black people in this country wanted what W. E. B. Du Bois so often pointed out over the course of his life—they wanted the freedom to work, the freedom to vote, and freedom from personal insult.

STEVEN TROUT: I've done a fair amount of scholarship on American commemoration of the First World War, and I'm very interested in the history of war memorials, but in this talk, I will go back to my roots as an English professor. Incidentally, I note that the gentleman to my right [Dr. Moten] has a bachelor's degree in English, and so we are a band of brothers up here, which is good. It's a relief to discover that I'm not the only person interested in literature here today.

What I would like to do is to quickly sketch out for you the southern literary response to the Great War, an extraordinarily rich and diverse response, and to talk about three specific southern writers. Two you are probably familiar with; the third you most likely are not.

Before doing that, however, I'd like to make a couple quick connections to some of the other presentations, which will bring some literary works into conversation with the history. We've been talking a lot today about African American experience in the South and overseas, and I want to mention two literary works from the twentieth century, each by an African American writer who hails from the South. The first is a book by a Tennessee writer who has the extraordinary name George Washington Lee, which reminds one of a certain college in the Shenandoah Valley. Born into a middle-class family, Lee was educated at Alcorn Agricultural and Mechanical College in Mississippi (today the historically black university Alcorn State), and in 1917, he qualified for officer training at the Fort Des Moines School that Professor Moten has told us about. Lee went on to serve in the Ninety-Second "Buffalo" Division in France, and after the war, he became a writer, businessman, and community leader in Memphis. In 1937, Lee published a novel called *River George*. This is the story of an African American soldier's return from the war, his homecoming. And one of the most interesting structural qualities of this novel is that it omits his war experience entirely. It's a bildungsroman, the history of a young man's development. It traces his life from early childhood to maturation, followed by his murder. He's lynched and, in the fashion that Dr. Williams spoke of, lynched in uniform. But his actual war experience is a huge void in the text, and I think this is quite deliberate. I think that Lee is saying something about memory, something about the place of the contributions of African American soldiers, combatants and noncombatants alike, in our national memory or within our national forgetting. So I recommend that book to you. It's not in print at the moment; however, it's a book that should be resurrected in a new edition at some point.

The second book dealing with African American experience and the First World War you're probably familiar with, and it is in my estimation the greatest African American novel of the twentieth century. I'm referring, of course, to Ralph Ellison's *Invisible Man*, published in 1952. Now, Ellison's *Invisible Man* would not qualify as a First World War novel per se, but this is nevertheless a work in which the war and its impact on people of color are extremely important. However, I should perhaps first back up and qualify my inclusion of Ellison as a southern writer. Ralph Ellison was born in Oklahoma, and like people in Missouri, my home state, Oklahomans are torn in terms of how they identify culturally and geographically. Some people in Oklahoma think of themselves as westerners or midwesterners. Others will identify as southern. Be that as it may, Ellison was fundamentally shaped by his later experiences in the Deep South, especially by his time at the Tuskegee Institute, founded by Booker T. Washington.

Invisible Man, a brilliant work of midcentury African American literature, tells the story, again, of a young man's development. It takes the unnamed protagonist, the Invisible Man of the title, from his roots in rural Alabama to the Tuskegee Institute and then on to Harlem. In the Tuskegee Institute portion of the book, he is charged by the president of the institute to take a member of the board of trustees on a sort of sightseeing tour of the campus and of the surrounding countryside, where he winds up running into a group of traumatized, shell-shocked African American veterans who are being "treated" in a brothel that is also a veterans' hospital. Clearly, this bizarre episode contributes to the hallucinatory quality of this work, which is decades ahead of its time in its postmodernity, but Ellison is also commenting on the separate but anything-but-equal healthcare afforded to black versus white veterans in the Deep South, and the scene ties in very much with some of the points that Professor Adler made in her presentation and that she has developed in her exciting new book. Ellison's novel also includes an interview between that member of the board of trustees and an African American physician who served in the American Expeditionary [AEF], and this is an exchange just bristling with energy and satire and insight, one that really sets the stage for a lot of what comes later in this complex and absorbing novel. So, if you've never read *Invisible Man* and were unaware of its connection with the memory and cultural legacy of the First World War, do check it out.

Finally, we've heard Professor Bristow's wonderful presentation on the Spanish flu epidemic and its impact on the South. There's a connection here too. I think one of the greatest literary depictions of the influenza epidemic is—and Professor Bristow knows where I'm going with this already—Katherine Anne Porter's short story "Pale Horse, Pale Rider," first published in 1939. Porter grew up in Texas. So, again, we have a writer who can be considered as both a westerner and a southerner. In the 1920s, she worked as an actress and as a journalist and editor in several different states and in Mexico. At the same time, she honed her skills as a creative writer. She is known especially for her short stories, and "Pale Horse, Pale Rider," her masterpiece, brings the Spanish flu pandemic to life like no other literary work I know. It tells the story of a romance between a woman journalist in Denver and an officer on his way to France. She catches the flu, nearly dies, and then comes out of her delirium only to discover that her lover caught the virus from her. He's dead by the time she becomes fully conscious. It's a heartbreaking story, beautifully told. (Incidentally, my grandmother on my father's side caught the flu in 1918, and if things had gone a little differently, I wouldn't be here today.)

Let me now turn to the three main writers I want to focus upon. After World War I, what's known as literary modernism, a movement that brings avant-garde experimentation to many different types of writing both in Europe and the United States, reached its zenith. Two modernist writers from the South really stand out. Both had voices that were operative on the national level and both captured the imagination of the reading public through their innovations with literary form. The first one is, of course, William Faulkner, arguably the greatest writer ever produced by the American South, and I always tell my students that if you're going to read just one book by Faulkner that engages with the memory of the First World War, that book should be *Flags in the Dust*. *Flags in the Dust*, which was published in 1976, is an extended and restored, posthumously published version of Faulkner's 1929 novel *Sartoris*, or if you prefer [southern accent] *SarTO-Ris*. (It always helps with Faulkner to read things aloud in a deep southern drawl because that's the way you hear them in your head.) Faulkner had to cut the original version of the novel considerably in order to appease his editor and to put the text into what was then regarded as "publishable form." In the 1970s, it was brought back in its full splendor. It's an absolutely riveting narrative, far superior, in my view, to *Soldier's Pay*, Faulkner's debut novel from 1924, which covers some of the same thematic territory with far less success. The first book to be set in Faulkner's fictional county of Yoknapatawpha, *Flags in the Dust* deals with a returning combat veteran, an aviator named Bayard Sartoris who has seen his twin brother, John, shot down in flames before his eyes. For the entire novel, the protagonist is enveloped in crippling survivor's guilt, and through his story, Faulkner provides an extraordinary study of psychological trauma caused by war.

He also does several other things that are fascinating. He manages to juxtapose the experiences of the Civil War ancestors in the Sartoris family and the heroic legends that have grown up around them with the experiences of Bayard in this ultramechanized conflict of 1914 to 1918. In the process, Faulkner winds up really questioning the validity of those southern heroic myths that were attached to the War Between the States. At the same time, he doesn't explore Bayard Sartoris's experiences in the conflict and afterward in isolation. He really has three veterans' voices operating within this text. For example, we meet an African American veteran by the name of Caspie, who talks at length about his wartime experience. Now, Caspie's voice is to some extent mocked in a novel that's upholding white supremacy, but at the same time, that voice is curiously empowered. Throughout Caspie's critique of the war and the things that he says about what he thinks is owed to him now that he has served the cause of democracy, there's enormous verbal energy (just like the verbal energy that goes into the Sartoris family's tall tales about the Civil War), as well as a thoroughly irreverent attitude toward whites. In other words, despite his comic treatment, Caspie creates some real tension in the novel's treatment of the connection between war and race. The third veteran in *Flags in the Dust* is my favorite: the Oscar Wilde–like decadent aesthete Horace Bimbo, who of all things was a YMCA secretary in France during the war. The way in which Horace was able to hide his decadence and hedonism behind the mission of the Young Man's Christian Association is obviously satirical, quite the jab at an organization that most American soldiers hated. So we have in *Sartoris* multiple perspectives on southern overseas service in the First World War, as well as an engagement with memory and history vis-à-vis the Sartoris family's ancestors in the Civil War and the stories told about them. This is a complicated, high-modernist text, but not nearly as difficult as some of Faulkner's other books. If you were put off by *The Sound and the Fury* when they made you suffer through that in high school, pick up *Flags in the Dust*.

The second modernist writer I want to just quickly note is, of course, William March. William March is the nom de plume for William Edward March Campbell, born in Mobile, Alabama, in 1893. March came from a large, hopelessly impoverished family. His father was a timber appraiser, whose job forced the family to move around constantly, and despite his obvious genius, March could never afford to complete a college degree. In 1917, he joined the Marine Corps and served, like Laurence Stallings (to whom I will turn in a moment), in the Marine Brigade of the AEF, earning the Distinguished Service Cross for heroism at the battle of Blanc Mont in 1918. After the war, March latched onto John Waterman, the head of a transoceanic steamship company headquartered in Mobile, and over the next fifteen years or so he improbably rose to a senior executive position in that company. In his spare time, he wrote fiction. His best-known novel is *Company K*, which has been reprinted with a fabulous introduction by Philip Beidler, who's at the University of Alabama. [Gesturing.] There's a copy of it over there by Dan Waterman. First published in 1933, this modernist work features 113 different narrators, each one of them a member of a fictional company in the Marine Brigade of the Second Division in the AEF. As we listen to the voices of these narrators, they take us from the enlistment of the soldiers in 1917 all the way through their service on the Western Front and in the Army of Occupation in postwar Germany. Members of Company K, those that survive, also tell us about their various homecomings in 1919, many of them bitter and tragic. March refused to see anything noble about war, and this extraordinary book hits you like a proverbial ton of bricks, as one story of brutality or heartbreak comes after another. If any of you have any particular questions about it, I'll be happy to talk with you about it during the Q&A. It's one of my favorites.

But first I want to take just a little more time to talk about a third major writer because while he's someone whose name you may have come across, you may not have necessarily thought about the extent to which his southern voice was important, particularly in the 1920s. This is a writer by the name of Laurence Stallings. Stallings was born into an upper-middle-class household in Macon, Georgia, in 1894 and then educated at Wake Forest University, where he majored in English. He enlisted in the Marine Corps in 1917, was commissioned as a second lieutenant, and then fought at the Battle of Belleau Wood in June 1918, where he was seriously wounded in both legs by German machine-gun fire. As a result of that wounding, Stallings went on—and here's another connection with your talk, Professor Adler—to write the first major work of American literature that deals with the theme of military disability. Published in 1924, his novel *Plumes* presents an autobiographical protagonist named Richard Plume, who, after being horribly wounded in both legs just like Stallings, attempts unsuccessfully to protest against the cultural glorification of war that led him to enlist. The book covers a number of themes. We learn, for example, of the generally indifferent care that Richard receives at the hands of the notorious Veterans Bureau in the early 1920s, and as with *Flags in the Dust*, the novel juxtaposes Richard's disillusioning experience of modern, industrialized warfare with family legends that celebrate military violence and southern manliness. It's a rich and fascinating book, and if you think about it, it introduces an entire genre that will later include other intimate depictions of wounding and disability, including Lewis B. Puller Jr.'s *Fortunate Son*, Ron Kovic's *Born on the Fourth of July*, and the depiction of Lieutenant Dan in the Robert Zemeckis film *Forrest Gump*.

After *Plumes*, Stallings went on to coauthor the single most important and most popular American play of World War I, *What Price Glory*, which premiered on Broadway in 1924. His coauthor was the playwright Maxwell Anderson. The two men met while working together for a newspaper in New York City. Notorious for its coarse language, which is actually toned down in comparison with real soldier's speech, *What Price Glory* ran for four hundred and some performances over a span of more than a year and a half, and it became a silent film in 1926. Stallings was involved in that production. In the 1950s, the play inspired a second film version, a vehicle for James Cagney, which some of you have probably seen. Following his stage success, Stallings was whisked off to Hollywood where he was asked by a film director, the silent-era auteur King Vidor, to create a one-page plot synopsis for a war film that was going to be called *The Big Parade* after one of Stallings's short stories. Released in 1925, *The Big Parade* became the second-highest grossing film of the silent era.

As you can see, Stallings was riding high in the mid-1920s. His career had him ricocheting back and forth between New York and Los Angeles, and he was a major player, I think it's safe to say, in the construction of American cultural memory of the Great War vis-à-vis theater and literature. He had a flop, however, in the late 1920s. He came up with an absolutely wretched theatrical adaptation of Ernest Hemingway's *A Farewell to Arms*, which was hated by Hemingway, along with just about everyone else. It tanked. After that, Stallings went underground for a while, but he reappeared in 1933, the year that Adolf Hitler assumed the Reich's chancellorship in Germany, and published an illustrated history of the First World War under the acerbic title, *The First World War: An Illustrated History*. This book, which is filled with all kinds of grotesque photographs of battlefield death and gore, each with a bitterly sardonic caption, was extremely controversial (and so it sold well), and it sparked a renewed cultural debate over what the supposed Great War for Civilization actually achieved. There were several prominent editorials about this issue inspired by Stallings's volume.

After the success of *The First World War*, Stallings worked for *Movietone News* and covered Mussolini's invasion of Ethiopia. During World War II, he worked in the Pentagon with the Marine Corps, probably engaged in military intelligence. In the 1950s he continued to write, and then in 1963, he published what is arguably his masterpiece, a book called *The Doughboys*. It's a 404-page history of the AEF. Historians today don't think much of it. I love it. I think it's a great book, especially in the colorful way it brings the personalities and legends of the Great War to life. I also think that through his blend of nostalgia and indignation Stallings captured the way that many American First World War veterans looked back on their war experience after nearly a half century. So, to conclude where Stallings is concerned, here we have a southern war writer whose career stretched all the way from the 1920s to the 1960s, almost up to the fiftieth anniversary of the armistice. He's a fascinating figure.

As I hope I've shown, more than a few southern writers wrote important works in response to the First World War. And it might even be fair to say that southern writers dominated literary representation of this conflict, playing a considerably larger role in the shaping of war cultural memory than their counterparts from other regions. American World War I literature is, to a large extent, southern literature.

AUDIENCE: I have a quick question for Dr. Jonathan Ebel about national civil religion. So, you were saying that the national civil religion and the southern civil religion are sort of developing at the same time. Have you come across any instances where the national religion not only differs from but sort of supersedes or maybe replaces part of the southern civil religion, or are they kind of coexisting, or is it more often that the national adopts the southern rather than the other way around?

EBEL: Well, I think in terms of the literature having to do with the Great War and the instances that I was referring to with the *Stars and Stripes*, there was a really concerted effort on the part of the authors and editors to assert the sanctity of the Union cause in the Civil War over and against the southern. So that would be one example. If you spend time in the American Battle Monuments–commissioned cemeteries in France, they are—I don't have any pictures to show you—they're the American cemeteries that have the white marble crosses everywhere, and in these cemeteries, there really is no regional identity. It's all national identity. The graves of Jewish soldiers are marked with Stars of David, but the overwhelming iconographic presence is that of crosses. So you have a kind of nationalist (read: northern) religious (read: Christian) depiction of the war and the war as lived and died, and so I would point to those as a couple of examples of that.

AUDIENCE: Two questions, one for Dr. Trout, one for Dr. Ebel. First, Dr. Trout, where would you put John W. Thomason in this and Thomas Boyd, where would you put those two in the whole literature of this kind of marine vets coming back and writing about their experiences? And Dr. Ebel: religious hand grenades? Is that what you said?

EBEL: Yes, religious history of the hand grenade. One of the ideas that I've had is to trace the intersection of religion and weaponry. It's a move that a lot of historians of religion have made to look at material culture, and if you're interested in war and the military, the material culture isn't simply memorial devices, it's also the devices that people wage war with. So I was interested in working on—I've kind of back-burnered this for the moment—a religious history of American warfare told in five or six weapons. And the hand grenade was especially interesting because it has become a site of sacrifice for the American soldier, actually the site of sacrifice par excellence. This is where one makes the supreme sacrifice and makes life possible for those around one. And clearly there's a strong intersection there with a religious understanding of soldiering and death in war. But it wasn't always that way. I mean, that ritual practice, that war practice, came from somewhere. In fact, in the Great War, I have not found a single instance of an American soldier dying because he covered a hand grenade. It's a learned behavior, so my questions are, "Where did that come from?" "Who's the first person to do it?" Because there's a first person. Someone started it, and then there's a narrative that developed from it. As best as I can tell, for American soldiers it's a National Guardsman from Neenah, Wisconsin, in World War II. There is one example of a British soldier who inadvertently dropped a grenade and covered it in World War I and died as a result of his injuries. A couple of instances in the *Stars and Stripes* of soldiers who put a foot over a grenade, but it wasn't the same sort of "using your body to shelter everybody" act that we think of today. It's also an interesting way into the intersection of war and sport, which has clear connections to the Muscular Christian movement of the late nineteenth and early twentieth centuries, so that's my thinking on that.

AUDIENCE: OK. I was thinking the Holy Hand Grenade of Antioch.

EBEL: Well, yes, I mean of course, no presentation on hand grenades is complete without a reference to Monty Python.

TROUT: You mentioned Thomason and you mentioned Boyd. Of course, Thomason wrote an extraordinary illustrated memoir called *Fixed Bayonets* that came out in 1925 or 1926. It was published by Scribner, the same publisher that would do Boyd's *Through the Wheat* and then later *Points of Honor*. I would simply say this, which isn't exactly responding to your question directly, but it's perhaps worth pointing out. The Marine Corps seems to have this uncanny ability to recruit really good writers. I don't think the Marine Corps does this intentionally, but if you look at the history of personal writings from American combatants in the twentieth century, it's pretty impressive. You've got March; you have Stallings; you have Thomason; you have Boyd—these are four prominent voices in the 1920s, all of them marines in World War I. The Marine Brigade at full strength in World War I only held nine thousand soldiers, so this is an extraordinary concentration of literary talent in a very small unit. Then you look at World War II; you look at

Robert Leckie's *Helmet for My Pillow*; you look at E. B. Sledges's *With the Old Breed*; you look at Sid Phillips's *You'll Be Sor-ree*; you look at something like Phil Klay's *Redeployment*. I just marvel at how much talent has been concentrated in the corps. They're more than just good at killing people, which is what marines will tell you.

AUDIENCE: Warrior poets, they like to be called.

AUDIENCE: I have a question for Steve, and I have a question for Derryn too. First of all, Laurence Stallings, I'm a big fan, and I saw other fans in the room, and I want to just highlight a point that you made, which is that here is a southern writer and his writings about treatment in the veterans' health system are really negative, and so this underscores the point that just because these facilities and this health system existed doesn't mean that people were happy with it and happy with their treatment. And so I wonder whether when you're reading him—and you mentioned he was a southerner and here we are in this conference about the South—do you think that his regional origins impact his perception of things like this federal system? I'm just thinking about it in terms of what I've learned in the last month or two, reading about the South and thinking about this increased presence of the federal government.

TROUT: Well, the way I think about that now has been impacted by what you've said today because now I'm thinking about Stallings coming from an environment in which the federal government did not have that great of a presence. Here we have an autobiographical character navigating a frustrating bureaucracy, and the way that the literal movement in that novel operates is that we go from the southern setting based in Wake Forest, and we spend a lot of time in that novel in Washington, DC, and Washington, DC, is the home of the bureaucrats and it's the home of the inhuman mechanisms of government that are out of touch with the needs of people on a local level. So I think those sorts of tropes fit exactly the context that you've painted about where the South is vis-à-vis healthcare for benefits after World War I. I think that that works together very well.

AUDIENCE: Yes, I never thought of him as a southerner. So I also just wanted to ask you as an English professor if you could talk to us about how you teach what you're talking about today, and how much—when you're teaching about memory of war—how much biography you include for your students, how much of that is you talking to students about the background of authors and how much is you encouraging them to find out about authors. I mean, we teach about representations of war, and even when we talk about historical monographs written by people in this room, our students ask, "Well, who is this person?" So I'm curious about as a professor who teaches literature how you handle that. And then just one question for Derryn, which is: I was very interested in the conclusion you were drawing about HBCUs or suggesting about HBCUs in the research you're doing on Alabama State, and I wonder if in this institutional history of your university, there's room for you and your department to draw larger conclusions about how Alabama State fits into the larger HBCU network and whether there's a much bigger story that's all about activism and advocacy on the campus of these colleges and universities.

MOTEN: I suspect that there is a larger sort of role, and I also suspect that it's connected. The challenge or the difficulty is finding the historical records. I know that we have five graduates of the Fort Des Moines Negro Officer Training School. I believe Tuskegee had twenty-five to thirty, which is a huge number. I suspect that there was communication between these campuses by faculty, by students, by presidents. I have a letter that I found in Robert Russa Moton's papers to Emmett Scott in Washington, DC, where Moton says that the "talk among negroes is that the hanging in Houston was a lynching." That's in the letter. And so this is not my sort of twenty-first-century reading into that. That's how Moton felt and how others felt in 1917 when that happened. I'm dying to know more, I really am, and I would like to draw those larger conclusions, but Emmett Scott's papers are at Morgan State University. Unfortunately, they're closed because they're not processed. There's some of his papers at the National Archives, but Morgan has the bulk of his papers. Moton's papers are at Tuskegee. Booker T. Washington has papers at the Manuscript Collection at the Library of Congress and also at Tuskegee. You know, there's some important papers at the Moorland-Spingarn Collection at Howard University. I think we can learn a lot about those wider sorts of notions, but I'm still digging.

TROUT: To respond to your question about the use of biographical information—or I'm assuming your question also extends to social-historical contextual information about literature—for me, it doesn't work to front-load it. How you historians can hold the attention of an entire class for fifty minutes or an hour and fifteen minutes by lecturing is astonishing to me. I can't hold their attention for ten minutes if I try to lecture, so what I do is I say, "Start reading this thing. I'm not going to tell you much about it, but you're all required to bring in ten questions" or whatever next time. You know, "What's something you don't understand about the world that this book is set in that you need to know?" And so if I'm teaching something like *Plumes*, usually the students are curious about the author anyway, as you indicated. So they'll say, "Hey, did this guy serve?" "Where did he serve?" "Was he wounded himself?" "What kind of care did he receive?" "How did he feel about the war?" He was in the Marine Corps. "What did the Marine Corps do in World War I?" "What was this Fourth Infantry Brigade that he was in?" So for me at least, with my teaching style, it's not that this will naturally come from the students. I kind of have to force it, but if I can make it an assignment like, "Hey, you're going to have ten questions about this text by whatever," then I can respond to those questions and it keeps the students more engaged than if I sort of give the overview before I present the work.

AUDIENCE: Are students curious about writers today, in your classroom?

TROUT: Yes, students are very, very curious about writers. They're very curious about writers, and we have a lot of writers at my university. We have a lot of students who are in our creative writing concentration, and so they read everything in terms of, "What can I take away from this as a creative person, and what was the creative process that this writer followed? I'm curious about that." So, I get that reaction quite commonly. But Derryn: I found your talk absolutely fascinating, and there's a dimension of it I wanted to hear some more of your comments on. It seemed to me that you had to work as a researcher to discover this extraordinary legacy and the issue of why World War I is regarded as the Forgotten War. One would have thought given that record of achievement and given that these individuals were coming from prestigious venues for people of color at that time, one would have thought that this would have been a treasured memory. Can you speak to that? Why it wasn't a treasured memory, or why you had to come along later at the centennial and research this? I'm really intrigued by that.

MOTEN: It's a great question, and I suspect that the reason why is that it was treated as a great memory at places like Howard University, Tuskegee University—but at the State Normal School, they were literally fighting for their lives, and so it just got subsumed in the minutia of day-to-day, of trying to survive. What I don't have, what I desperately want is something from the staff, the faculty, the students, talking about their pride in these five graduates of this school. And you know, this was a big, big deal, having this officers' training school is a huge achievement for these historically black schools. And I know—or I shouldn't say "I know"—I strongly suspect that there was a great deal of pride in it, but again, the records are just sketchy. I have nothing, or I have found nothing, at our university that even talks about how the five students that graduated from our campus were recruited. I suspect it was the president, but I don't have evidence of that.

Notes

1. "Kiffin Rockwell, World War I Aviator," Virginia Military Institute, www.vmi.edu.

2. Kiffin Rockwell, *Letters of Kiffin Rockwell, Foreign Legionnaire and Aviator, France, 1914–1916, with Memoir and Notes by Paul Ayers Rockwell* (Garden City, NJ: Country Life Press, 1925), 56.

3. "Courts-Martial Sentences at Present Merely Military Commands," *Congressional Record* 27 (January 1919): 2109–10.

4. "Soldiers Found Guilty of Houston Riots: Execution Is Carried Out in Secret," *Miami (OK) District Daily,* December 11, 1917.

Afterword

Remembering the Great War

JAY WINTER

This book forms part of the global array of centenary reflections on what Europeans call the Great War and what Americans call World War I. Over the past five years, the 1914 to 1918 conflict was marked or recalled by millions of people throughout the world as a global war that transformed the lives of individuals and of families, as much as the destiny of nations. Many of these commemorative projects focused on the traces the war left on the regional and local levels. This shift from the imagined community of the nation to the community of direct, lived experience of towns, cities, farms, and factories brought millions of people into commemorative activity not on the battle-fields of Europe but where they lived.

Historians are part of the commemorative landscape, but we swim in a stream we did not create and do not control. The reason is that the Internet revolution has created a space in which very large numbers of people share stories about the Great War, alongside other wars. Online archives exist to an extent never before known, enabling everyone with an interest and access to a computer to consult a vast array of historical sources on the war and to exchange stories about the war with a wide array of people. The Internet privileges visual sources, and photographs by the millions may be consulted by a very large population fascinated by the Great War. There are reenactment societies in the United States, like those all over the world, who use the Internet to get together with other enthusiasts, to buy period items with varying degrees of authenticity, and to stage First World War battles.

To be sure, these reenactments are fake history. But to the enthusiasts, who try to be as accurate as possible as to the cloth and insignia on uniforms and the weapons and kit soldiers used, they are engaged in living history, whereas we professional historians, through our detachment and insistence on sources, produce cold history. I can see the attraction of reenactment for those who believe they can actually relive the past. It quickens the pulse of people living mundane lives. But whatever it does for practitioners, reenactment falsifies the past. No one can reenact battle without blood and shit and terror, and middle-aged men running through a field lack even a modicum of respect for what real soldiers actually did on the battlefields of the Great War, or any other war. They lack respect, too, for the dead, which is the real source of the obscenity of reenactment.

What can we historians do about the First World War equivalents of *Confederates in the Attic*? We can do what we have always done; we can tell the truth about the war with as much documentation and compassion as we can.

Dixie's Great War shows how important the writing of history is to commemoration. Commemoration without history risks sliding into infotainment or costume drama. And yet we cannot become purists, saying that we do history but we don't do memory. That is not a viable option. We historians live in societies and serve them.

For all too long, we professionals have followed an older tradition that treats memory and history as if each were isolated majestically on their separate peaks. The truth is otherwise. Memory and history overlap; each is impossible without the other. In a nutshell memory is history seen through emotion, affect, feelings. History is memory seen through documents and the narratives we build on them. History has procedures of confirmation and disconfirmation. Historians can prove that something didn't happen in the way that someone else says it did. False memories are harder to contradict, but sometimes historians can persuade people that what they remember did not take place. What we cannot do is turn our backs on memory, as if it were a communicable disease.

Both history and memory create narratives about the past, and they overlap in important respects. Most historians choose a subject in history for reasons related to their family origins. They may not admit it, but most of those I know take conversations about the past circulated around the dinner table—what Jan Assmann calls communicative memory[1]—and store them away in a form that pops up when the time comes to choose a research subject or frame an argument. Historians inject their personal memory into their research, simply because they live in societies and families and not only in archives.

On the other hand, what historians or novelists write or what filmmakers portray tends to enter our memory landscapes. That is true both for individuals and for groups. For the latter, we need to turn to sociologist Maurice Halbwachs, a pioneer in constructing a category beyond individual memory.

He called that category "collective memory," or the memory of collectives, who knew who they were by the stories they told.[2] Families are such collectives, and their activities in naming a child tell him or her about the collective memory of his or her birth. We are never the first to know who we are, Halbwachs affirmed; somebody told us our name.

Halbwachs insisted that we make sense of our memories by references to the groups that matter to us. When the groups change—through divorce, disease, migration, or death—when they do not come together to tell the story of who they are, then collective memory vanishes. He never equated collective memory with national memory. For him, nations don't remember, groups of people do when they come together in public to do the work of remembrance.

Over the last thirty years, historians of memory have sketched out a path based on a simple distinction. Memory is the product of a long process of individual reflection and of social interaction. That process we call remembrance. It means that in some places, groups of people do the work of memory in public. When they so gather, they produce collective memories, those formed by a group in action. We all have individual memories, sitting in our armchairs. But we share collective memories when we do something with other people that marks important events in the past—like World War I.[3]

Using this framework, it makes sense to pose the following questions. What has characterized the collective memory of World War I in the American South, and how does the writing of history relate to it?

The answer the contributors to this book provide is that the collective memory of World War I in the American South overlapped with that of the country as a whole, but that the nature of southern society framed the collective memory of the South in particular ways. A racially segregated society remembered the Great War through the prism of race. The same was true in many parts of America, but in the South, that prism had facets related not only to slavery, but to the Civil War, emancipation, occupation, and the creation of a postbellum society with its own racial hierarchy in those states that joined the Confederacy.

What this book demonstrates is that while the collective memory of white southerners and black southerners diverged, the history they shared is one. There was a moment in the discussion (p. 80) when a member of the audience spoke of his memories and asked the historians whether they concurred. They did not. Here are the views of a member of the audience: "I grew up as a southerner the first twenty-five years of my life in a segregated society, so that's my reality. I would classify most southerners as believing in the concept of separate but equal as opposed to white 'supremacy.' I'm just wondering what your experience is with this and whether you make that kind of distinction as you view the morality of attitudes past." None of the historians agreed. Their job was to test memories against documents, and they affirmed that white "supremacy" was at the core of "separate but equal." Here is historian Chad Williams's reply: "We are talking about a set of practices, a set of ideas, that is thoroughly ingrained and institutionalized throughout the US military and comes directly out of the particular history and social and political realities of black life in the South. So I understand sensitivity to that term [white supremacy], especially nowadays, but it's real, and I think it aptly characterizes the nature of the military in the context of World War I and perhaps aptly characterizes the nature of the American nation as a whole." Here is a clear instance of the way historians can say that, alongside memories, realities existed that can be documented, interrogated, even proved. Historians, after all, are in the truth business; I am not suggesting that the member of the audience I cited spoke untruths. Instead he spoke from the collective memory of his early life as a southerner. When memory and history clash, we have to turn to the documents we have to resolve the tension between them. And that is precisely what the historians contributing to this volume have done.

A second question arises from this exchange between speakers and listeners. Questions about race and the racial divide appear repeatedly in this book. The question that follows is whether World War I changed race relations in the South in any significant way. The answer is complex and includes divergent tendencies. On the one hand, military service by three hundred thousand African Americans did not bring them closer to winning their civil rights. Indeed, the spike in lynchings in 1919 suggests that racial violence worsened when white people confronted the specter of the return home of so many black men trained to fight. On the other hand, black men both at home and abroad moved in circles they could never have known without wartime mobilization. Furthermore, the arrival of federal money for war-related projects benefited everyone and provided a focus for protest and agitation for equal rights. Two steps forward and two steps backward may sum up this mixed story of the effect of the war on racial inequality in the South, as elsewhere in the United States.

Some of the scholars who spoke in this series went further, opening up the possibility of a linkage between military service and the Harlem Renaissance in the 1920s. *We Return Fighting* is the title of an exhibition opened at the National Museum of African American History and Culture in Washington in late 2019 on the black experience in World War I. The title comes from W. E. B. Du Bois and places World War I in a long line of struggles leading to the civil rights movement of the post–World War II decades and beyond. The problem with this kind of history is that it arrays events in the past in a positive, progressive direction, one that was hard to see at the time. Sometimes this kind of history is called "Whig history," derived from nineteenth-century British historians who showed that the past led inexorably to the glorious and benign present.

The problem with a history of progress is that it enables us to look at suffering and hardship and oppression as sacrifices for a better future. It is redemptive history, finding a shape in the past to give us hope in our struggles for a better future. What is missing in this kind of history is a sense of tragedy. The tragedy that the black men who died in the Great War did not die to make the world safe for democracy. They did not even make America safe for democracy.

The central problem of writing the history of World War I is that its narrative pales in comparison to that of the Civil War and to that of World War II. Both became wars of liberation, the first from slavery and the second from fascism. Who was liberated by World War I? Poles, Finns, Latvians, Lithuanians, Estonians, even Armenians for a time, though almost all these liberated peoples succumbed to the monsters to the west or to the east. It is difficult to find a narrative that is sufficiently heroic for the First World War to compete with the big wars that came before or after.

Yes, American involvement in the First World War was short, and the toll in lives lost on the battlefield was much, much smaller than those in the Civil War or the Second World War. For these reasons, stories about World War I were not as deeply braided into family history as were stories about the men and women of 1861 to 1865 or 1941 to 1945. But the central reason why Dixie's Great War or that of the United States is still relatively unknown is that the 1917 to 1918 war does not fit into a story either about the long road to racial equality or about the emergence of America as a hegemonic power. World War I lacks the heroic elements needed to enter into the national narrative; the peace settlement that followed it failed completely, in part because of the failure of the US Senate to ratify it. There were heroes in that war to be sure. Think of Sergeant York, for instance. But wars are never as noble as many of the men who fight in them. They are nasty and stupid and cruel and leave countless victims in their wake. That is why a tragic approach to war suits this country, as much as it does every other country.

The only way to get there is to abandon the road-to-salvation approach to the study of the past. The scholars who put this book together have shown the way forward. Their story is full of grey tones, of half-chances, of disappointments, of letdowns, of callousness, of the betrayal of those men of color in uniform treated like dirt when they came home after the war. I take from these exchanges and arguments a sense that they point to a tragic view of war, a recognition that war is a Pandora's box, which when opened lets loose forces that punish victors and vanquished alike. Writing that kind of history is a task that awaits to be done.

NOTES

1. Jan Assmann and John Czaplicka, "Collective Memory and Cultural Identity," *New German Critique*, no. 65, Cultural History/Cultural Studies (Spring–Summer 1995): 125–33.

2. Maurice Halbwachs, *On Collective Memory*, ed. by Lewis Coser (Chicago: University of Chicago Press, 1959).

3. See Jay Winter and Emmanuel Sivan, "Setting the Framework," in *War and Remembrance in the Twentieth Century*, ed. Winter and Sivan (Cambridge: Cambridge University Press, 1999), 1–30.

Suggested Readings

This is a partial list of works on America in the Great War, selected either because they were produced by our panelists, cited by them in their comments or our introduction, or seemed relevant to our particular focus on the South and southerners.

Overviews/State Histories

Bettez, David J. *Kentucky and the Great War: World War I on the Home Front.* Lexington: University Press of Kentucky, 2016.

Downs, Matthew L., and M. Ryan Floyd, eds. *The American South and the Great War, 1914–1924.* Baton Rouge: Louisiana State University Press, 2018.

Kennedy, David M. *Over Here: The First World War and American Society.* 25th anniversary ed. New York: Oxford University Press, 2004.

McKinley, Shepherd W., and Steven Sabol, eds. *North Carolina's Experience during the First World War.* Knoxville: University of Tennessee Press, 2018.

Olliff, Martin T., ed. *The Great War in the Heart of Dixie: Alabama during World War I.* Tuscaloosa: University of Alabama Press, 2008.

Polston, Michael D., and Guy Lancaster, eds. *To Can the Kaiser: Arkansas and the Great War.* Little Rock, AR: Butler Center Books, 2015.

Rainville, Lynn. *Virginia and the Great War.* Jefferson, NC: McFarland, 2018.

Winter, Jay, ed. *The Legacy of the Great War: Ninety Years On.* Columbia: University of Missouri Press, 2009.

Commemoration and Culture

Budreau, Lisa M. *Bodies of War: World War I and the Politics of Commemoration in America, 1919–1933.* New York: New York University Press, 2010.

Ebel, Jonathan H. *Faith in the Fight: Religion and the American Soldier in the Great War.* Princeton, NJ: Princeton University Press, 2010.

————. *G.I. Messiahs: Soldiering, War, and American Civil Religion.* New Haven, CT: Yale University Press, 2015.

James, Pearl, ed., *Picture This: World War I Posters and Visual Culture.* Lincoln: University of Nebraska Press, 2009.

Kingsbury, Celia Malone. *For Home and Country: World War I Propaganda on the Home Front*. Lincoln: University of Nebraska Press, 2010.

Trout, Steven, ed. *Memorial Fictions: Willa Cather and the First World War*. Lincoln: University of Nebraska Press, 2002.

———. *On the Battlefield of Memory: The First World War and American Remembrance, 1919–1941*. Tuscaloosa: University of Alabama Press, 2010.

———. *Points of Honor: Short Stories of the Great War by a US Combat Marine (Thomas Boyd)*. Tuscaloosa: University of Alabama Press, 2018.

Race and Ethnicity

Barbeau, Arthur E., and Florette Henri. *The Unknown Soldiers: Black American Troops in World War I*. Philadelphia: Temple University Press, 1974.

Brown, Nikki. *Private Politics and Public Voices: Black Women's Activism from World War I to the New Deal*. Bloomington: Indiana University Press, 2006.

Ford, Nancy Gentile. *Americans All! Foreign-Born Soldiers in World War I*. College Station: Texas A&M University Press, 2001.

Keith, Jeanette. *Rich Man's War, Poor Man's Fight: Race, Class, and Power in the Rural South during the First World War*. Chapel Hill: University of North Carolina Press, 2004.

Laskin, David. *The Long Way Home: An American Journey from Ellis Island to the Great War*. New York: HarperCollins, 2010.

Lentz-Smith, Adriane. *Freedom Struggles: African Americans and World War I*. Cambridge, MA: Harvard University Press, 2009.

Mjagkij, Nina. *Loyalty in Time of Trial: The African American Experience during World War I*. Lanham, MD: Rowman and Littlefield, 2011.

Shenk, Gerald E. *"Work or Fight!" Race, Gender, and the Draft in World War One*. New York: Palgrave Macmillan, 2005.

Slotkin, Richard. *Lost Battalions: The Great War and the Crisis of American Nationality*. New York: Henry Holt, 2005.

Sterba, Christopher M. *Good Americans: Italian and Jewish Immigrants during the First World War*. New York: Oxford University Press, 2003.

Whalan, Mark. *The Great War and the Culture of the New Negro*. Gainesville: University Press of Florida, 2008.

Williams, Chad L. *Torchbearers of Democracy: African American Soldiers in the World War I Era*. Chapel Hill: University of North Carolina Press, 2010.

Zeiger, Susan. *In Uncle Sam's Service: Women Workers with the American Expeditionary Force, 1917–1919*. Ithaca, NY: Cornell University Press, 1999.

Diplomacy and the State

Fry, Joseph A. *Dixie Looks Abroad: The South and U.S. Foreign Relations, 1789–1973*. Baton Rouge: Louisiana State University Press, 2002.

Kennedy, Ross A. *The Will to Believe: Woodrow Wilson, World War I, and America's Strategy for Peace and Security*. Kent, OH: Kent State University Press, 2009.

Knock, Thomas J. *To End All Wars: Woodrow Wilson and the Quest for a New World Order*. New York: Oxford University Press, 1992.

Neiberg, Michael S. *The Treaty of Versailles: A Concise History*. New York: Oxford University Press, 2017.

Home Front Politics and Society

Capozzola, Christopher. *Uncle Sam Wants You: World War I and the Making of the Modern American Citizen*. New York: Oxford University Press, 2008.

Gibbs, Christopher C. *The Great Silent Majority: Missouri's Resistance to World War I*. Columbia: University of Missouri Press, 1988.

Huebner, Andrew J. *Love and Death in the Great War*. New York: Oxford University Press, 2018.

Kazin, Michael. *War against War: The American Fight for Peace, 1914–1918*. New York: Simon and Schuster, 2017.

Neiberg, Michael S. *The Path to War: How the First World War Created Modern America*. New York: Oxford University Press, 2016.

Tippens, Matthew D. *Turning Germans into Texans: World War I and the Assimilation and Survival of German Culture in Texas, 1900–1930*. Kleingarten Press, 2010.

Veterans, Medical Care, and Humanitarianism

Adler, Jessica L. *Burdens of War: Creating the United States Veterans Health System*. Baltimore: Johns Hopkins University Press, 2017.

Bristow, Nancy K. *American Pandemic: The Lost Worlds of the 1918 Influenza Pandemic*. New York: Oxford University Press, 2017.

Irwin, Julia F. *Making the World Safe: The American Red Cross and a Nation's Humanitarian Awakening*. New York: Oxford University Press, 2013.

Kinder, John M. *Paying with Their Bodies: American War and the Problem of the Disabled Veteran*. Chicago: University of Chicago Press, 2015.

Linker, Beth. *War's Waste: Rehabilitation in World War I America*. Chicago: University of Chicago Press, 2011.

Ortiz, Stephen R. *Beyond the Bonus March and GI Bill: How Veteran Politics Shaped the New Deal Era*. New York: New York University Press, 2010.

Women and Gender

Cobbs, Elizabeth. *The Hello Girls: America's First Women Soldiers*. Cambridge, MA: Harvard University Press, 2017.

Dumenil, Lynn. *The Second Line of Defense: American Women and World War I*. Chapel Hill: University of North Carolina Press, 2017.

Ebbert Jean, and Marie-Beth Hall. *The First, The Few, The Forgotten: Navy and Marine Corps Women in World War I*. Annapolis, MD: Naval Institute Press, 2002.

Gavin, Lettie. *American Women in World War I: They Also Served*. Boulder: University Press of Colorado, 1997.

Grayzel, Susan R., and Tammy M. Proctor, eds. *Gender and the Great War*. New York: Oxford University Press, 2017.

Jensen, Kimberly. *Mobilizing Minerva: American Women in the First World War*. Urbana: University of Illinois Press, 2008.

Kennedy, Kathleen. *Disloyal Mothers and Scurrilous Citizens: Women and Subversion during World War I*. Bloomington: Indiana University Press, 1999.

Kuhlman, Erika. *Of Little Comfort: War Widows, Fallen Soldiers, and the Remaking of the Nation after the Great War*. New York: New York University Press, 2012.

Vuic, Kara Dixon. *The Girls Next Door: Bringing the Home Front to the Front Lines*. Cambridge, MA: Harvard University Press, 2019.

Conscription, Combat, and Soldiers

Ball, Gregory W. *They Called Them Soldier Boys: A Texas Infantry Regiment in World War I*. Denton: University of North Texas Press, 2013.

Bristow, Nancy K. *Making Men Moral: Social Engineering during the Great War*. New York: New York University Press, 1996.

Frazer, Nimrod T. *Send the Alabamians: World War I Fighters in the Rainbow Division*. Tuscaloosa: University of Alabama Press, 2014.

Grotelueschen, Mark Ethan. *The AEF Way of War: The American Army and Combat in World War I*. New York: Cambridge University Press, 2007.

Gutiérrez, Edward A. *Doughboys on the Great War: How American Soldiers Viewed Their Military Experience*. Lawrence: University Press of Kansas, 2014.

Keene, Jennifer D. *Doughboys, the Great War, and the Remaking of America*. Baltimore: Johns Hopkins University Press, 2001.

———. *World War I: The American Soldier Experience*. Lincoln: University of Nebraska Press, 2011.

Lengel, Edward G. *To Conquer Hell: The Meuse-Argonne, 1918*. New York: Henry Holt, 2008.

Truss, Ruth. "The Alabama National Guard at Home and Abroad, 1914–1919." In *The Great War in the Heart of Dixie: Alabama during World War I*, edited by Martin T. Olliff, 24–40. Tuscaloosa: University of Alabama Press, 2008.

Webster, Anne L., ed. *Mississippians in the Great War: Selected Letters*. Jackson: University Press of Mississippi, 2015.

Contributors

JESSICA L. ADLER, an assistant professor of history and health policy and management at Florida International University, researches and teaches about US health and social policy, war and society, and American political development. Her first book, *Burdens of War: Creating the United States Veterans Health System* (Johns Hopkins University Press, 2017), is about the World War I–era origins of the nation's largest integrated health care system. Her current projects examine late twentieth-century transformations in the veterans' medical system and health care in US prisons. Adler's work has been supported by the Rockefeller Archive Center, the Friends of the Princeton University Library, the National Endowment for the Humanities, the Florida Humanities Council, the Doris G. Quinn Foundation, the Institute for Political History, and the US Army Military History Institute.

NANCY K. BRISTOW is a professor of history at the University of Puget Sound, where she also serves in the African American Studies Program and on the leadership team of the Race and Pedagogy Institute. She is the author of three books, including *Making Men Moral: Social Engineering During the Great War* (New York University Press, 1996) and *American Pandemic: Lost Worlds of the 1918 Influenza Epidemic* (Oxford University Press, 2012). Her third book, *Steeped in the Blood of Racism: Black Power, Law and Order, and the 1970 Shootings at Jackson State College* (Oxford University Press, forthcoming) was released in May 2020. Bristow is continuing her exploration of social cataclysm and memory with her current project, a broad study of state violence against African Americans during the Black Power era.

JONATHAN H. EBEL is a professor in the Department of Religion at the University of Illinois, Urbana-Champaign. He specializes in the religious history of the United States and has written on the role religion plays in shaping American soldiers' war experiences and the nation's war memories. Ebel received his BA from Harvard in 1993 and his PhD from the University of Chicago in 2004. He served as a naval intelligence officer from 1993 to 1997 and continued in that capacity in the naval reserves until 2005. Ebel is the author of *G.I. Messiahs: Soldiering, War, and American Civil Religion* (Yale University Press, 2015) and *Faith in the Fight: Religion and the American Soldier in the Great War* (Princeton University Press, 2010). He also coedited *From Jeremiad to Jihad: Religion, Violence, and America* (University of California Press, 2012) with Prof. John Carlson of Arizona State University. He was a Guggenheim Fellow for 2017–18.

JOHN M. GIGGIE is associate professor of history and African American studies at the University of Alabama, where he also serves as director of the Summersell Center for the Study of the South. He is the author of *After Redemption: Jim Crow and the Transformation of African American Religion in the Delta, 1875–1917* (Oxford University Press, 2008), coeditor of *Faith in the Market: Religion and the Rise of Commercial Culture* (Rutgers University Press, 2002), coauthor of *America Firsthand* (2010, 2013, 2015), and coauthor of *The Unfinished Nation* (McGraw-Hill Higher Education, 2018). He is currently preparing a book on civil rights protests in West Alabama. He received his PhD from Princeton University.

ANDREW J. HUEBNER is professor of history at the University of Alabama. He is the author of *Love and Death in the Great War* (Oxford University Press, 2018), *The Warrior Image: Soldiers in American Culture from the Second World War to the Vietnam Era* (University of North Carolina Press, 2008), and coauthor of *The Unfinished Nation* (McGraw-Hill Higher Education, 2018). He earned his graduate degrees in history from Brown University and in 2017 was named an Organization of American Historians Distinguished Lecturer.

JENNIFER D. KEENE is a professor of history and dean of Wilkinson College of Arts, Humanities, and Social Sciences at Chapman University. A past president of the Society for Military History, she has published three books on American involvement in the First World War: *Doughboys, the Great War and the Remaking of America* (Johns Hopkins University Press, 2001); *World War I: The American Soldier Experience* (University of Nebraska Press, 2011), and *The United States and the First World War* (Taylor and Francis, 2000). She is also the lead author for an American history textbook, *Visions of America: A History of the United States* (Pearson, 2016) that uses a visual approach to teaching students US history. She has received numerous awards for her scholarship, including Fulbright Senior Scholar Awards to France and Australia and a Mellon Library of Congress Fellowship in International Studies. She served as an associate editor for the *Encyclopedia of War and American Society* (Sage Publishing, 2005), which won the Society for Military History's prize for best military history reference book. She coedited, along with Michael S. Neiberg, *Finding Common Ground: New Directions in First World War Studies* (Brill, 2011). She has published numerous essays and journal articles on the war, served as a historical consultant for exhibits and films, an associate editor of the *Journal of First World War Studies*, and as a general editor for the "1914–1918-online," a peer-reviewed online encyclopedia and major digital humanities project.

ROSS A. KENNEDY is professor of history and chair of the History Department at Illinois State University. He is the author of *The Will to Believe: Woodrow Wilson,*

World War I, and America's Strategy for Peace and Security (Kent State, 2009), which won the Scott Bills Prize in Peace History. He also edited *A Companion to Woodrow Wilson* (Wiley-Blackwell, 2013) and has written extensively on American domestic politics and foreign policy during World War I. Kennedy's current project, entitled "The United States and the Origins of World War II," analyzes how the policies of the United States contributed to the structure of Great Power politics from 1918 to 1939.

DERRYN MOTEN was born in and grew up in Gary, Indiana. He received his BA in English from Howard University, MS in library science at Catholic University of America, MA in American studies from the University of Iowa, and PhD in American studies at the University of Iowa. He serves as the chair of the History and Political Science Department at Alabama State University; copresident of AFT Faculty-Staff Alliance, AFL-CIO, Alabama State University; vice chair on AFT Higher Education Policy and Planning Council; and southern vice president of Alabama AFL-CIO.

MICHAEL S. NEIBERG is the inaugural chair of war studies in the Department of National Security and Strategy at the US Army War College in Carlisle, Pennsylvania. His published work specializes on the First and Second World Wars, notably the American and French experiences. The *Wall Street Journal* named his *Dance of the Furies: Europe and the Outbreak of World War I* (Harvard University Press, 2011) one of the five best books ever written about the war. In October 2012 Basic Books published his *The Blood of Free Men*, a history of the liberation of Paris in 1944. In May 2015 Basic published his *Potsdam: The End of World War II and the Remaking of Europe*, which won the Harry S. Truman Prize. In October 2016, Oxford University Press published his *Path to War*, a history of American responses to the Great War from 1914 to 1917, and the next year, *The Treaty of Versailles: A Concise History*.

MARTIN T. OLLIFF received his PhD in US history from Auburn University in 1998. He was assistant university archivist at Auburn from 1996 to 2002 then, in 2002, became director of the Wiregrass Archives at Troy University Dothan Campus, where he is now a professor of history. He edited *The Great War in the Heart of Dixie: Alabama during World War I* (University of Alabama Press, 2008) and authored *Getting Out of the Mud: The Alabama Good Roads Movement and State Highway Administration, 1898–1930* (University of Alabama Press, 2017). He has been president of the Alabama Historical Association, the Alabama Association of Historians, and the Society of Alabama Archivists and has sat on the board of directors of the Alabama Historical Commission and Alabama Humanities Foundation as well as the editorial boards of the *Alabama Review: A Quarterly Journal of Alabama History* and *Provenance: The Journal of the Society of Georgia Archivists*.

STEVEN TROUT is chair of the Department of English at the University of Alabama. He has authored or edited twelve books, including *On the Battlefield of Memory: The First World War and American Remembrance, 1919–1941* (University of Alabama

Press, 2010), *Memorial Fictions: Willa Cather and the First World War* (University of Nebraska Press, 2002), and *World War I in American Fiction: An Anthology of Short Stories* (coedited with Scott D. Emmert, Kent State University Press, 2014). He is an historical adviser to the US World War I Centennial Commission and a member of the Alabama World War I Centennial Committee. He also edits the book series War, Memory, and Culture for the University of Alabama Press.

RUTH SMITH TRUSS is professor of history, former chair of the Department of Behavioral and Social Sciences, and current interim dean of the College of Arts and Sciences at the University of Montevallo in Alabama. She received her PhD from the University of Alabama with a focus on military history. Ruth is the author of several journal articles on the Alabama National Guard and of "The Alabama National Guard at Home and Abroad, 1914–1919" in *The Great War in the Heart of Dixie: Alabama in World War I*, ed. Martin T. Olliff (University of Alabama Press, 2008). She is also the coeditor with Dr. Sarah Wiggins of *The Journal of Sarah Haynsworth Gayle, 1827–1835* (University of Alabama Press, 2013).

KARA DIXON VUIC is the LCpl. Benjamin W. Schmidt Professor of War, Conflict, and Society in Twentieth-Century America at Texas Christian University. She is the author of *The Girls Next Door: Bringing the Home Front to the Front Lines* (Harvard University Press, 2019), and *Officer, Nurse, Woman: The Army Nurse Corps in the Vietnam War* (Johns Hopkins University Press, 2010). She is the editor of *The Routledge Handbook on Gender, War, and the U.S. Military* (2017) and coeditor of the University of Nebraska Press's series Studies in War, Society, and the Military.

CHAD L. WILLIAMS is the Samuel J. and Augusta Spector Professor of History and African and African American Studies and chair of the African and African American Studies Department at Brandeis University. He specializes in African American and modern US History, African American military history, the World War I era, and African American intellectual history. His first book, *Torchbearers of Democracy: African American Soldiers in the World War I Era* (University of North Carolina Press, 2010), won the 2011 Liberty Legacy Foundation Award from the Organization of American Historians, the 2011 Distinguished Book Award from the Society for Military History, and designation as a 2011 CHOICE Outstanding Academic Title. He is coeditor of *Charleston Syllabus: Readings on Race, Racism and Racial Violence* (University of Georgia Press, 2016) and *Major Problems in African American History* (Cengage Learning, 2018, 2nd ed.). He has published articles and book reviews in numerous leading journals and collections, and his public writings have appeared in venues such as *Time*, the *Washington Post*, the *Conversation*, and *Black Perspectives*. He has earned fellowships from the Radcliffe Institute for Advanced Study at Harvard University, the American Council of Learned Societies, the Schomburg Center for Research in Black Culture, the Ford Foundation, and the Woodrow Wilson Foundation.

JAY WINTER, the Charles J. Stille Professor of History Emeritus at Yale and honorary professor at the Australian National University, is a specialist on the First World War and its impact on the twentieth century. He is a founder of the Historial de la Grande Guerre, the first comparative museum of the First World War, in Péronne, Somme, France. In 1997 he received an Emmy award as coproducer of the eight-hour BBC/PBS television series *The Great War and the Shaping of the Twentieth Century*, screened in twenty-eight countries. Winter is the author of *Sites of Memory, Sites of Mourning: The Great War in European Cultural History* (Cambridge University Press, 1995), *War beyond Words: Languages of Remembrance from the Great War to the Present* (Cambridge University Press, 2017), and editor of the three-volume *Cambridge History of the First World War*, published in 2014 in English and French and in Chinese in 2019. He has received honorary doctorates from the University of Graz in 2010, the Catholic University of Leuven in 2014, and the University of Paris in 2015. In 2017 he received the Victor Adler Prize of the Austrian state for a lifetime's work in history.

Index

www.ingramcontent.com/pod-product-compliance
Lightning Source LLC
Chambersburg PA
CBHW031939090426
42811CB00002B/238